The Dillon Companies Flight Department

A Brief History

1948?—2014

Researched & Compiled

By

Michael W. Sims

Copyright © 2024 Michael W. Sims

ISBN:979-8-3306-7261-5

Cover Photo: Dillon Stores Archives

Cover design, book design & layout by:

The author, Ray E Dillon III., Steve Dillon & Henry Platts

Acknowledgments

The following people generously contributed to this book.

Paul Dillon: Gave the author access to the Dillon Stores Archives, providing photos and historical content.

Ray E. "Butch" Dillon III: Provided photos and historical content of his father's military service and other images and content.

Henry Platts (Ace's Grandson): Editor of the book and provided content.

Doug Crow (Gary Crow's Son): Photos and content.

Dean Wedman: Photos.

Chuck Montgomery: Photos and content.

Roger Humiston: Photo and content.

Lincoln Hall: Content.

The Hutchinson News: Articles and photos.

Steve Harmon: Historical composition advisor.

Wayne Fagan: Howard 500 facts & Photos

Dedication

This book is dedicated to my family. My wife, Carolyn Sue (Susie) and two daughters, Julie Ann and Amanda Jo. They stood by me and endured my absence at times during special occasions as I pursued my childhood dream of being a pilot. Also, to the good people at Dillon Companies Inc. who provided a pathway to fulfill my dream in my hometown. This is rare in today's business aviation environment. And to all the men and women who aspire to or are involved in business aviation. There are no set schedules and at times long hours and multiple days away from home. But the job is very gratifying in knowing you have in some way been a part of your company's success.

FORWARD

From its humble beginnings as a general store opened by J.S. Dillon in Sterling, Kansas, in the 1890s, the company expanded to open its first cash food market in Hutchinson in 1913. It was incorporated in 1921 as J.S. Dillon and Sons Stores with stores in surrounding communities, becoming Dillon Companies Inc. in 1968 with many subsidiaries to its present-day part of the Kroger Company.

But only a few individuals are aware of its global reach with its flight department. The company had a worldwide presence through its Wells Aircraft subsidiary under the guidance of Ray E. "Ace" Dillon Jr. and William "Bill" Haines.

Business aviation got its start in the 1920s when cabin-class airplanes made their debut. Enclosed cabins meant protection from the elements as opposed to the open cockpits of earlier types. The advantages were no wind in your face, a quieter ride, and, of course, heat.

The Dillons might not have used aircraft for business before WWII, but they were familiar with their use. Ray Dillon Sr.'s brother and Paul Dillon's father, Clyde Dillon, was lost in Colorado while on a hunting trip in 1940. Ray Dillon Sr. and the family hired a Twin Beech from Wichita, Kansas, to search for him. They spent many days scouring the area from the air and ground. Unfortunately, he was not found until the following spring. Clyde had succumbed to the harsh winter environment of the Colorado Rockies.

The Dillons recognized the utility of the airplane, and in 1946, Ray Dillon came up with a promotional idea to fly a plane loaded with California produce to Hutchinson for sale in the stores. To maximize the effect, it was scheduled to correspond with the Kansas Flying Farmers convention being held in Hutchinson in May of that year.

California Eastern Airways refrigerated DC-4.

Dillon's first air cargo of fresh fruits and berries landed at Hutchinson Airport on May 24, 1946. Over 225 planes lined the runways at Hutchinson Municipal Airport on this date during the Kansas Flying Farmers Convention.

Unloading operations are underway in this photo.

A large gathering attended the significant event, warmly welcomed by Mr. and Mrs. Dillon (Ray, crouching beside the sign on the right, and Stella, the first woman on the right), alongside notable figures of the era. These included Mayor Bell and Mrs. Bell, Chamber of Commerce President Max Wyman and Mrs. Wyman, Chamber of Commerce Secretary Bert Snyder and Mrs. Snyder, and Beth Wyse, owner of Radio Station KWBW.

Table of Contents

Acknowledgments iv

Dedication... v

FORWARD vi

Chapter One: The Beginning:Post-WWII 1

Chapter Two: The 1950's Expansion Continues. 14

Chapter Three – The 1960's – Onto Bigger & Better Things 23

Chapter Four: The 1970's Soaring Times! 59

Chapter Five: The 1980's More Growth with Kroger......................96

Chapter Six: The 1990's A Changing Landscape........................123

Chapter Seven: The New Millennia 135

Epilogue.. 142

External Links   144

Chapter One:
The Beginning: Post-WWII

Ray E. "Ace" Dillon Jr.

1st Lt. Ray E. 'Ace' Dillon Jr., U.S. Army Air Corps, 492nd Fighter Squadron, 48th Fighter Group, Ninth Air Force, served valiantly in the European theater during World War II as a skilled pilot of the Republic P-47 fighter planes.

Republic P-47 "Thunderbolt"
Photo by Tim Felce ⧉ #1

Ace entered the US Army Air Corps in February 1943 and shortly thereafter was sent to Flight School in Tullahoma, Tenn, at William Northern Army Air Corp base.

**Ace's Stearman PT-17 #333
"Kaydet"**

Boeing Aircraft Co. Stearman built the Primary Trainer PT-17, which became a subsidiary of Boeing in 1934. The PT-17 was also called the Boeing Stearman or "Kaydet". There were 10,600+ built.

The Kaydet was sturdily built to withstand the rigors of student training. Sitting on a conventional gear (tail wheel) design with tandem open cockpits, the student is in front, and the instructor is in the rear.

The United States Navy trained many pilots in the PT-17 at the Hutchinson Naval Air Station. One of the Navy Instructors, Earl (Red) Baughman, was employed at Wells Aircraft for a time, but for medical reasons, not as a pilot.

After the war, thousands of PT-17's were sold as surplus. They were used as crop dusters, sport planes, and stunt flying/wing walking in air shows.

Sent overseas in Aug. 1944, Ace was stationed in England, Belgium, and Germany. Ace served in the Ardennes battle, the Rhineland campaign, and central European operations.

"Betty 1"

This is the first P-47 Ace flew in combat. Notice the name of Ace's wife, Betty, just forward of the cockpit canopy. Unfortunately, it was lost in a crash while being flown by another pilot when Ace was on leave.

Ace was issued a second P-47, which he promptly and proudly named Betty 2nd.

Ace on the wing of "Betty 2nd."

Ace had one close call when German anti-aircraft artillery shrapnel hit Betty 2nd.

Ace kept this piece of shrapnel for posterity.

Ace completed 92 combat missions during eleven months of deployment.

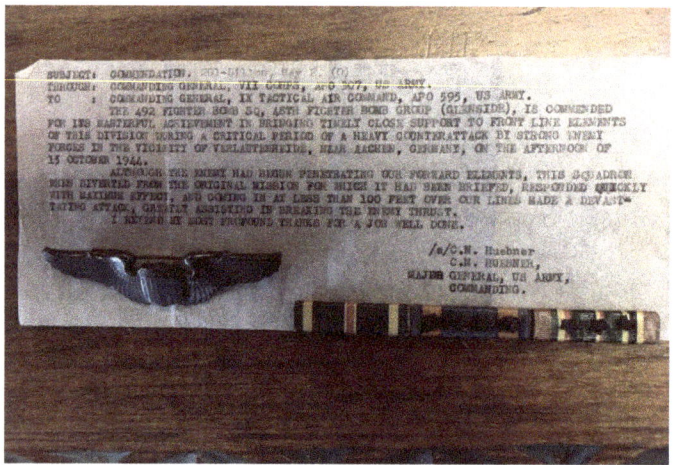

Commendation For Mission Flown 15 Oct 1944

The commendation reads as follows:

SUBJECT: COMMENDATION. 201 – DILLON, RAY E. (0)

THROUGH: COMMANDING GENERAL, VII CORPS, APO 307, US ARMY.
TO COMMANDING GENERAL, IX TACTICAL AIR COMMAND, APO 595, US ARMY.

The 492 fighter bomb sq, 48th fighter bomb group (Glenside), is commended for its masterful achievement in bringing timely close support to front-line elements of this division during a critical period of a heavy counterattack by strong enemy forces in the vicinity of Verlautenheide, near Aachen, Germany, on the afternoon of 15 October 1944.

Although the enemy had begun penetrating our forward elements, this squadron when diverted from the original mission for which it had been briefed, responded quickly with maximum effect, and coming in at less than 100 feet over our lines (authors note: with eight 50 cal. Machine guns firing) made a devastating attack, greatly assisting in breaking the enemy thrust.

I extend my most profound thanks for a job well done.

/a/C.N. Huebner

C.N. HUEBNER,
MAJOR GENERAL, US ARMY,
COMMANDING.

Ace was awarded the Distinguished Flying Cross and Air medal with twelve clusters.

Distinguished Flying Cross

Awarded for: "Heroism or extraordinary achievement while participating in an aerial fight."

Bronze Air Medal

Awarded for: "Meritorious achievements while participating in actual combat in support of operations."

Ace kept his medals, commendation, and the piece of shrapnel in a drawer of his bedside table as a testament to his mettle and a source of motivation.

Upon his return to the US in July 1945, many believed that Ace had acquired the nickname "Ace" due to his service in the Army Air Corps. However, this was not the case. He was a very active and devoted Boy Scout, earning the highest level of scouting as an "Eagle Scout." He had to write a story and read it to his fellow scouts to earn one of his merit badges. He wrote about an "ace" pilot from WWI. After his presentation, one of the other scouts said, "We should call you 'Ace,'" and the nickname stuck. During his time in the Army Air Corps, he never divulged his nickname "Ace" to his fellow airmen!

Ace demonstrated an early interest in flying and airplanes. In his youth, he actively engaged in building and flying model airplanes.

Ace's Cousin Paul and younger brother Dick also served in the military. Paul served in the US Navy and remained overseas for 15 months. He participated in the invasion of Borneo and the liberation of the Philippines.

Dick joined the Army Air Corp post-war. He was stationed at Harlingen and San Antonio Texas army airfields. Because of a surplus of pilots after the war, Dick was not sent to flight school.

Paul Dillon   **Richard "Dick" Dillon**

Both learned to fly following World War II. The exact time they started flying for company business remains unclear, but it's believed to have been in the mid to late 1950s or early 1960s.

Following his discharge from the Army Air Corps in September 1945, Ace resumed his career in the family business. At this time, the company was growing, as was Ace, in responsibility and vision for the future. Recognizing the value in using private airplanes as "Time Machines", Ace began flying himself and other executives to various store locations. Thus, the "Dillon Flight Department" was founded.

At first, it was just Ace as the pilot, renting airplanes from Wells Aircraft of Hutchinson, Yingling Aircraft, and United Beechcraft of Wichita.

Ace continued to fly for business and personal purposes until he was well in his 70s.

Following WWII, the company expanded to more cities in central and western Kansas, and in 1948 or 1949, Dillons bought its first plane, a Beechcraft Bonanza. The Bonanza, introduced in 1947, featured all-metal construction, seating for 4, and retractable landing gear. It was fast for its time and instantly recognizable for its unique "V" tail design. Over time, the Bonanza evolved. More powerful engines were installed for more speed. It grew to a 6-seater but lost its distinctive "V" tail. Regardless, it is still being built to this day.

The Dillon Stores first airplane.

This photo was taken on Wells Aircraft's ramp looking northeast.
The Dillon Logo is barely visible behind the rear window.
Notice that the primary color is yellow, which was the background color used in the Dillon Stores logo during this era. Today, this color is no longer in use. This airplane is the only known Dillon aircraft to feature yellow in its paint scheme. Later, it became known that Ace despised the color yellow. Consequently, in the following years, anyone who suggested using yellow on an airplane faced Ace's wrath!

This is the same Bonanza.
Why this photo is not in color is not known but the Dillon logo is more discernable.

Wells Aircraft

Wells Aircraft was established in 1928 by Roland Wells. Wells was a barnstormer during the era between the World Wars, which included the great depression. A barnstormer performed stunt flying and giving airplane rides at various locations to earn money.

Roland Wells – circa the 1920s or 1930s boarding a Laird "Swallow" airplane.

Wells's business was located in the first hangar built at the Hutchinson Municipal Airport. There were two buildings located south of and joined to the hangar. They served as offices for Wells and airline agencies. The ramp in front of the hangar was the only one available for civilian use until the 1950s.

Hutchinson Municipal Airport circa 1930s.

Roland survived those early years and the depression by barnstorming, flying the mail for the U.S. Postal Service, flying charters, giving flying lessons, and buying, selling, and maintaining airplanes.

Roland Wells in the early 1940s beside his Piper J-5 "Cub Cruiser."

After WWII, Wells started dealing in Globe Swift and Luscombe aircraft.

Photo courtesy of Chris England
Globe Swift

The Globe Swift was a two-seater little hot rod with retractable landing gear and all-metal construction. The Swift model GC-1A first flew in 1942.

**Photo courtesy of Chris England
Luscombe 8E "Silvaire"**

The Luscombe Aircraft Co. was founded in 1933 and introduced its most popular model, the two-seater 8A, in 1937. It is not known if Ace rented and flew these airplanes or not. But, being a "fighter pilot," most money says he did!

The purchase of the yellow Bonanza and its stationing at Wells Aircraft inadvertently made Wells Aircraft the "Home" of the Dillon Flight Department, which would expand in the coming years.

The Dillons Bonanza shared a home with other notable, established Hutchinson company planes. Among those was William D.P. Carey's personal airplane, a Beechcraft E-18. Mr. Carey was the founder of Packaging Corporation of America. Collingwood Grain Co. operates several grain elevators in the area, a Cessna 310. Borton Co. Inc., commercial building contractors, Beechcraft Baron & Cessna 310. Western Foods, manufacturers of condiments and pickles, a Beechcraft Bonanza. Other company airplanes based there were flown by company pilots, their owners, Roland Wells, or contract pilots.

Ironically, after he retired, the company Roland Wells founded would be the base for a Hollywood production company making a movie about a barnstormer!

Two of the early contract pilots are profiled in the following pages.

Contract pilot Robert "Bob" Bowman, 1950.

Bowman, a WWII vet, served as a naval aviator attached to Pearl Harbor squadron 44. Bowman flew the Consolidated Aircraft PBY "Catalina" flying boat. PB was designated for Patrol Bomber, and the Y was for the manufacturer. Squadron 44 flew the "Black Cats" painted black for night deployment in the southwest Pacific. Bowman was also a flying instructor at the San Jose, CA, Naval Air Station. As a civilian, he was employed by Yingling Aircraft Services of Wichita and later as a contract pilot. Bowman remained a contract pilot for Wells, Dillons, and many other companies until his passing in late 1973.

Consolidated PBY "Black Cat"
Photo by the U.S. Navy ©

Contract pilot William "Billy" Powell, 1960.

Another contract pilot, William "Billy" Powell, was a local pilot who farmed in western Reno county. His background as a pilot is unknown, but it is believed to have been military. He held a commercial pilot certificate with instrument and multi-engine ratings. He flew with Wells, Dillons, and others into the 1970s. Mr. Powell passed away in August of 2018.

Chapter Two: The 1950s Expansion Continues.

As the '50s began, Dillon Stores had several locations in Kansas. With the success of those locations, Ray Dillon Sr., President and CEO Ace, and other members of the Dillon family and management began to think bigger. New stores in Kansas were built.

Most of the expansion was in central Kansas and the city of Wichita. But the area was also growing to the west. Roads in Kansas during this time were narrow and sometimes gravel, making them treacherous at times. There were also no direct routes, which made them time-consuming. This made the airplane more and more valuable as a "time machine."

Note: The following articles and (3) photos were taken from the 1951 editions of the company publication "The Dillonair," a monthly internal news magazine featuring company changes, personnel accomplishments, promotions, and other pertinent social information.

Van Camp Seafoods Inc. of Terminal Island, California, producers of *Chicken of the Sea* tuna have entered the frozen food field by producing a tuna pie. The first pies to be made under the Chicken of the Sea label came out Monday, February 15, 1951, and were flown directly to Dillon's in Van Camp Seafood Company's giant PBY "Catalina" amphibious airplane from Omaha, Nebraska. J. S. Dillon & Sons received 1,000 cases in this first shipment. The shipment was delivered to Dillons by Mr. Gordon Curtis, sales manager for Van Camp Seafood Inc., who piloted the company plane with the history-making first shipment. Mr. Curtis returned to California with the company plane after a brief visit with Dillon officials.

Van Camp also valued the airplane not only for transportation but also for finding schools of tuna and promotional purposes.

What better way for the Chicken of the Sea Company than to travel in a corporate conversion of a Consolidated Aircraft PBY naval patrol bomber and advertise at the same time, as illustrated in the following 1951 photo of a visit to Dillons.

Pictured from left to right: John Crawford, grocery buyer and secretary treasurer of Dillons, Ralph Whitmer of McManus – Heryer Brokerage Co. Charles Schmucker, Dillon's merchandise buyer, Jim Garrigus, district sales representative for Chicken of the Sea Tuna, Al Niles, of McManus – Heryer Brokerage Co., Gordon Curtis, sales manager/pilot for Chicken of the Sea Tuna and Ray Dillon, President of Dillon Stores.

The Van Camp's PBY has quite a history behind it as it was the first Navy plane to sight the Japanese fleet as it approached the island of Midway preceding the battle of Midway in WWII. The Japanese attacked it and sustained over 20 bullet and shrapnel holes as evidence of its encounter. According to the log, one of the gunners was killed in the fight. At that time, it was under the command of Ensign Long. This airplane was portrayed as "Strawberry 5" in the original movie "Midway."

Ace has taken an active position with the firm since his return from the Army Air Corps following WWII five years ago. Ace is an assistant to his dad and is also the chief pilot of the Dillon Company's Bonanza.

The Dillon Stores second Bonanza of the early 1950's.
Note the larger Logo on the side.

Bonanza #3
Ace enters the airplane, followed by his father, Ray.
The company Logo is no longer displayed.

Note: In anticipation of growing Airline service, a new airline terminal, air traffic control tower, and restaurant were built in 1954 at what is now the east end of 11th. Ave. Also, in the mid-fifties, runway extensions were taking place. Continental Airlines was now flying the new British built Vickers "Viscount" airliner powered by four-turboprop engines, ushering in the Jet Age to Hutchinson.

The new terminal now displays Hutchinson Municipal Airport, and the old terminal that Wells Aircraft occupies now displays Wells Aircraft Sales.

Always seeking ways to expand, significant changes came in 1957.

The Kroger Grocery Company was a major competitor in central Kansas. As Dillons grew and became more successful, a deal was struck with Kroger to sell all 16 of its Wichita Division stores to Dillons. This moved the Dillon stores further into central and southeastern areas of the state.

As the Company grew, so did Ray Dillon Sr's acquaintance with other grocery company owners. One of those owners was Lloyd King of King Soopers of Denver, Colorado. Ray and Lloyd began discussing the advantages of a merger should the economic conditions in either geographic area become distressed. One company could sustain the other during difficult times, so it was decided to merge the two companies.

As the company grew, it became evident that Ace could not fly every required trip. Ray Dillon Sr. sometimes used Yingling Aircraft or United Beechcraft to fly him on trips when Ace and/or the Bonanza were unavailable. On one such trip, Ray asked then-contract pilot Robert "Bob" Bowman if he could recommend anyone available for the Company to hire as a full-time pilot. Bowman told Ray he had just the right guy, a talented pilot from the area. So, sometime in 1957, the company hired a young man named William F. "Bill" Haines, who grew up on a farm south of Hutchinson, to be a full-time pilot and be responsible for the care of the aircraft.

Wm. F. "Bill" Haines – age 19.

This photo was taken as he prepared to fly then-Kansas Governor Arn to Topeka in the spring of 1951.

Due to the acquisition of King Soopers, the company acquired its first Beechcraft model 18, "Twin Beech." It was a modified "D" model which basically was the civilian version of the military C-45 transport. The Dillon airplane had a fuel-fired heater instead of the engine exhaust heat muff type used on the C-45. It also had an "airstair" door that hinged at the bottom and incorporated steps for entering. The standard "D" utilized an oval-shaped door that hinged toward the front and was a challenge getting into for some people!

The Dillon's Beech 18

Introduced in 1937, the model 18 was Beechcraft's first entry into the twin-engine cabin class airplanes. It was fast and dependable and powered by two Pratt & Whiney R-985 radial engines. Aimed primarily at America's growing airlines and private industries as an executive transport, it was hugely successful. During WWII, the military also used the 18 as a navigator, bombardier trainer, and utility transport. It was in continuous production in various forms for 32 years, being retired in 1969.

The flight department becomes more valuable as a time saver. The "18" is now being utilized quite often with the addition of King Soopers and the acquisition of the Kroger stores.

Wells Aircraft and Dillon Co. would utilize various models of the "18" well into the 1980s. One was believed to have been Olive Ann Beech's personal tricycle gear version of the "18", one of the last built-in 1969. Its tail number was "N177X."

The significance of this number will be revealed in later chapters.

Some of Dillon's suppliers also utilized the "Twin Beech." This photo was taken in the early 1950s when the Stokely-Van Camp Company visited Dillons.

Near Disaster!

A frightening incident occurred sometime after the "18" was put into service. Paul Dillon relates that Haines and Ray Dillon were returning from somewhere in Missouri when Ray noticed smoke in the cabin. Haines determined it was a cabin heater problem and eliminated the cause of the fire by shutting down the left engine since fuel for the heater was supplied by its fuel pump. But insulation and interior materials continued to smolder in the cabin, producing a toxic environment. Haines opened the cockpit windows to eliminate the smoke, but it was too intense. Ray opened the cabin airstair door, which promptly blew off the airplane when the safety chain failed! Fortunately, Ray was holding on tight and was not blown out, but it was a close call. Fortunately, the now free door did not strike the tail of the "18," causing the plane to be uncontrollable. Haines landed safely in Kirksville, MO. Both were shaken, but neither were seriously injured in the incident.

With the Kwik Shop's division of Dillons being envisioned and developed in the late '50s, the future of the flight department would be growing along with the Dillon Stores.

With the first Kwik Shop built at the Southeast corner of 30th Ave. and Plum Street in Hutchinson, Dick Dillon, Ace's younger brother, serves as Director of Kansas Stores Operations and put in charge of future development.

This was the start of the Dillon convenience store division.

Chapter Three – The 60's – Onto Bigger & Better Things

At the beginning of the decade, three fixed base operators (FBOs) were at the Hutchinson Municipal Airport. All were located on the West side of the airfield. FBOs were service providers for general aviation; they did not fly scheduled routes.

Operators of scheduled routes were called "Airlines," now referred to in aviation circles as "Scheds." Each was governed by different FAA (Federal Aviation Administration) rules.

The three FBOs at the airport at the time were:

Wells Aircraft, the largest of the three, operated by Roland Wells, was located at the far south end of "Hangar Row." Wells provided charter services, known at the time as "Air Taxi" service, flight instruction, pilot service, aircraft maintenance, and sales.

Case Flying Service, operated by Hershel Case, was located north of Wells. Case provided some of the same services as Wells but on a much smaller scale.

Sparks Aviation, operated by Frank Winters, was located north of the Kansas Army National Guard hanger which was located between Case and Sparks.

In 1958-59, the City of Hutchinson, which is the governing agency of the airport, built two storage hangars just north of a private hanger leased to Security Grain Co., which was located just north of Sparks. The purpose of these hangers was to provide storage for privately owned aircraft as Wells, Case, and Sparks were fully occupied. The city also was the only provider of aviation fuels, utilizing city employees and equipment for this service.

In January 1960, a new FBO, Skycraft Inc., appeared. They were operated by Robert "Bob" Armstrong and Lorance Bloom. On February 1, 1960, a lease agreement was entered with the city and Skycraft Inc. to operate an FBO. The firm took over the storage hangers and fuel sales at that time. Wells, Case, and Winters were not happy as the new business may draw some business from them and, to add insult to injury, they now had to purchase their fuel from a competitor!

1962: Ray Dillon Sr. and the Board of Directors appointed his son Ray E. (Ace) Dillon Jr. as president of J. S. Dillon & Sons Stores Co., Inc.

Ray Dillon Sr. is now Chairman of the Board of Directors & CEO, Ray Dillon Jr. is President & COO, Dick Dillon is Director of Kansas Stores & Kwik Shops, and Ray E. Dillon Sr's—nephew Paul Dillon Secretary-Treasurer of the company.

Ace was now certified to fly "Airplane" single-engine and multi-engine land with an instrument pilot rating.

Dick was certified to fly "Airplane" Single Engine & Multi Engine Land.

Paul was certified to fly "Airplane" single-engine land.

1964 saw a significant change at Wells Aircraft. Roland Wells had decided to retire and sell the operation. At the time, the two biggest customers of Wells were the Dillons and William D.P. Carey of Packaging Corp. of America. The Dillons had Bill Haines as pilot and custodian of the Dillon Airplanes, while Carey had Jay Frizzo as pilot and custodian of his airplane.

Haines and Frizzo did not want an outsider in control of Wells. They were concerned it could mean changes in policy and personnel. So, Haines and Frizzo went to their bosses and tried to convince one or both principals to purchase the operation with one or both pilots as manager/managers.

Their pleas were acknowledged. Ray Dillon and William Carey were friends, and they devised a plan to buy Wells together. They formed Wells Aircraft Inc. with total stock shares of 50. Each purchased 25 shares, the value of each share determined by the purchase price to Roland Wells.

Mr. W.D.P. Carey

Mr. Carey was the founder and first president of Packaging Corporation of America (PCA). It was formed in 1959 by the merger of three companies. Those three companies comprised other small companies, including the Carey Straw Mill (aka the Straw Board Co.) of Hutchinson. PCA merged in mid 60's with Tenneco.

Carey's pilot, Jay Frizzo, was a WWII vet who participated in flying "The Hump" in C-46s over Burma.

Mr. Carey's Beech E18

With the acquisition of Wells by Dillon and Carey, this opened some doors for Ace and Haines!

Haines had learned from Roland Wells that money was to be made buying and selling airplanes. Because Globe and Luscomb had gone out of business by this time, Haines convinced Ace they should take on an aircraft dealership. This took some doing as the manufacturers were very protective of their dealerships, allowing only one in some geographic regions.

At the time, Skycraft Inc. had the Cessna dealership with a strained agreement with Yingling Aircraft of Wichita. Yingling held the Cessna distributorship for most of Kansas and had its dealership at

Wichita's Mid Continent Airport. Ironically, Mr. Robert "Bob" Armstrong, co-founder and President of Skycraft, was a salesman for Yingling. When Mr. Yingling learned of Armstrong's plan to open his own business, he was livid! Somehow, a deal was made, and Skycraft got its dealership. Some speculate that Cessna Aircraft became involved because its Hydraulics Division was located just Southwest of the Hutchinson airport. Cessna of Wichita and Hutchinson had an Employees Flying Club. Those members in Hutchinson had to drive to Wichita to participate in the club's benefits. When learning of Armstrong's proposal, it's believed Hutchinson's Flying Club members petitioned Cessna to grant Armstrong's request.

Coincidentally, at the time, Ray Dillon Sr. was on the Board of Directors of Cessna Aircraft!

A Beechcraft dealership was not an option as they had their own dealership network, "United Beechcraft Inc." with locations scattered across the Country. And, of course, one in Wichita. Beech did grant some individual dealerships in high-density areas, such as "Executive Beechcraft" of Kansas City.

Frank Winters of "Sparks Aviation" held the Piper Aircraft Corp. dealership as an associate of an unknown entity.

This left Mooney Aircraft of Kerrville, Texas. Haines knew the Mooney dealer in Wichita. Aero Services Inc. was owned and operated by Ulysses "Rip" Gooch. Gooch had the Mooney distributor rights for Kansas and a portion of Missouri. Aero Services facilities were located on Rawdon Field just north of Beech Field and their manufacturing facilities. Beech was on the south side of Central Ave., and Rawdon was on the north. Beech had a nongovernment air traffic control tower, and for safety purposes, both Beech field and Rawdon field used the Beech Air Traffic Control facility.

Ulysses L. "Rip" Gooch

Ulysses Gooch was an African American WWII veteran. Although not a pilot during the war, he began learning to fly shortly after. In time he earned his commercial and flight instructor ratings. Being black, he had little luck finding a job in aviation. He worked part-time as a stunt flyer with airshow organizer and performer Bill Sweet for a while.

Rip moved to Wichita, "The Air Capital of the World", in 1951. In the late '50s, after battling racism in non-flying jobs, Rip started his own business. Well-known as the founder/owner/operator of Aero Services, he was one of the first black-owned modern FBOs in the U.S., which provided a stepping-stone for other black pilots.

Rip's aviation career spanned 37 years. He also served in many political appointed and elected positions. He served on the Kansas Commission on Civil Rights from 1971 to 1974. At the time, one of the few blacks was elected to the Wichita City Council from 1989 to 1992, including two one-year terms as vice mayor and elected as a Kansas State Senator, serving from 1993 until 2004 with many committee assignments. Rip earned many honors in both his aviation and political careers. He was well-liked, admired, and respected by all who knew him.

The Mooney that Paul Dillon flew was purchased from Aero Services.

Although it is not known how profitable the Mooney dealership was for Wells, Wells had two for demonstration purposes and was used by Dillons. However, this gave Wells credentials as an aircraft dealer and opened many doors for Haines!

During the mid-60s, Haines met several dealers and characters from around the USA and other countries.

Such as:

Jack Adams Sr. and Jr. from "Two Jacks Aircraft Sales" operate their business in Little Rock, AR, West Memphis, AR, and Olive Branch, MS.

Tal Miller of Denver Co.

Blaine Gardner of Manila, Philippines.

Jan Mann of Phoenix, AZ.

Henry Seale of Dallas, TX

Dee Howard of San Antonio, TX.

Roy Gilbreath of Dallas and San Antonio, TX. (Worked with both Seale and Howard.)

Jimmy Alexander of Wichita.

And others, one notable Harry Swanton!

More about these individuals to follow.

Also, with the formation of Wells Aircraft Inc., James "Jim" Hephner was hired as lead mechanic. Hephner possessed the qualifications Roland Wells had regarding inspection authority when Wells retired. Roland had employed two or three mechanics when he retired, but none had the advanced qualifications required. Hephner was a rigorous guy and demanded perfection from those he was in charge of!

**Hephner's vision of a "Real Aircraft Mechanic"!
Pictured in flight at a few thousand feet,
Photo by Bill Larson ⌕ #2**

The company expanded into western Arkansas, Missouri, and eastern Oklahoma, establishing a regional headquarters in Fayetteville, Arkansas. As the Kwik Shop division extended into other parts of the state, Nebraska, and Iowa, management determined the need for more than one twin-engine airplane. Consequently, they traded Bonanza #3 for a Cessna 310, which entered service in the mid-1960s.

**Cessna 310-K
Photo by Alan Wilson ⌕ #3**

A Mooney M20 was also purchased sometime in this era. It was smaller than the Bonanza and was used primarily by Paul Dillon. It was also a speedy 4-place retractable landing gear airplane. With a distinctive tail design referred to as reverse swept or the "backward tail." It is still being built today.

Paul Dillon and the Mooney.

With the addition of the Cessna 310, management decided that Wells Aircraft should hire a full-time pilot to assist with the Dillons and Mr. Carey's airplanes. Chosen was another local fellow named Steve Wanasek. Before Wells hired him, Steve was an avid aviation fan who bought and restored an old dismantled Aeronca "Chief" at his parent's property at the Northeast corner of Hendricks Street and 17th Ave. After the restoration and against his parents' wishes, Steve taxied the plane across 17th Ave. into an open field and took off! Steve flew his "Chief" to Hutchinson Municipal Airport and took it to Wells. Steve had learned to fly at Wells, where Wells's mechanics inspected it and certified it airworthy. Steve then took it to Strickler's airfield, a grass airstrip west of Hutchinson, where he kept it until it was sold to a local flying club.

Aeronca "Chief"
Phot courtesy of Chriss England

The Dillon fleet now consisted of the Beech 18, Cessna 310, the Moony, and a Cessna 195 (described later in this chapter).

Another Near Disaster!

Paul Dillon and another company exec, Al Wagler, also a pilot of WWII and a pilot of some of the company's planes, were returning from Arkansas in the Moony when they encountered thunder storms. Unable to avoid them as they were growing around them, Paul and Al experienced severe turbulence before emerging from the storms. After a safe landing in Hutchinson, Paul and Al described their ordeal to Haines and the aircraft mechanics at Wells. Upon inspection of the Moony, it was discovered that the turbulence had sprung the wing spar on one side of the plane, and that wing was five inches higher at the wingtip than the opposite side. Had the plane's wing been exposed to much more turbulence, it may have failed, resulting in fatalities to the occupants!

However, as the company grew during the '60s, Paul's duties required him to be more and more office-bound. Since he was flying less, Haines and Paul became concerned about his proficiency. After discussing the matter, it was mutually agreed that Paul should give up flying as a pilot and be flown by a professional pilot. This allowed him to devote his time to company responsibilities.

Wagler, "Big Al," as he was called, continued to fly the company airplanes until the fleet became all turbine powered.

Aircraft Engine Service

Aircraft Engine Service, established by Sylvan Lair, was an aircraft engine overhaul and parts business specializing in radial, "round" engines. They also rebuilt opposed cylinder, "flat" engines on a smaller scale.

Roland Wells had been using Aircraft Engine Service (A.E.S) for rebuilt radial engines and parts for some time. A.E.S was less costly than other rebuilders and closer to Hutchinson, located at Wiley Post Airport of Bethany, OK, a northern suburb of Oklahoma City. Before the jet age, most larger airplanes were powered by radial engines. Radial engines powered the Dillons, Careys and other Wells Aircraft customers' airplanes.

Haines was familiar with A.E.S. and liked Sylvan Lair. Sometime in the mid-60s, talk of a partnership developed, and soon thereafter, A.E.S. became a subsidiary of Dillon Stores. Haines was now the liaison for Dillon Stores and A.E.S.

Also, around this time, Haines became acquainted with other aircraft dealers from around the country and one from the Philippines, Blaine Gardner (hereinafter referred to as Gardner).

Gardner was a WWII Army Air corps vet based in Manila after Gen. MacArthur retook the Philippines in July 1944. Gardner liked the Philippines and returned there after being discharged from the Army Air Corps and establishing a flying service. His company served the Philippines and the southeast Asian countries thereby.

After WWII, oil exploration was booming in the Western and Southwestern Pacific area, and Gardner landed contracts with many exploration companies. He began buying large twin-engine military airplanes that had been converted for civilian use in the USA. These airplanes were fast, long ranged, and able to cross long stretches of water. In addition to himself, Gardner had several pilots in his employ. Among them were Bob Holt and Harry Swanton. It is believed that Holt had served with Gardner in the service, but it is known that Swanton had been based in Guam, flying reconnaissance in PBYs. Swanton and Bowman did not know each other until after the war.

The author does not know how Haines and Gardner became acquainted, but it could have been through other dealers Haines had done business with or perhaps through A.E.S. They liked each other, and Gardner quickly became a long-time customer of Wells Aircraft. However, a half-generation apart, Gardner became a good friend of Haines's.

One of their first transactions involved a North American B-25 converted for civilian use. Wells was to inspect the aircraft pre-purchase and confirm it met all FAA Airworthiness Directives. On board the aircraft were Gardner, Harry Swanton, and a (name unknown) mechanic. This was the first time Haines had met Swanton.

Swanton was a large, boisterous, and outspoken man; you knew when he was on the property! He was, however, a very congenial and gentle man to work with. While in the service, he was noticed by Hollywood producers filming war documentaries. His outgoing personality earned him an invitation to Hollywood to do screen tests to see if he could become an actor after leaving the service. Sadly, he could not. However, it was determined that he would be a perfect 'stand-in' for John Wayne because of his size!

As they worked with each other, Swanton and Wayne became close friends and drinking buddies. Occasionally, their drinking got them into trouble, and at one time, they got into a fistfight with each other! After taking many hits, kicks, and falls for Wayne making movies, Swanton said, "To hell with this." He'd had enough and wanted to return to flying for a career. He learned that Gardner was looking for a PBY pilot and went to work for him. He and Wayne, however, remained close friends.

Bowman and Swanton, despite never having met before Swanton's arrival in the B-25, shared a unique connection; Swanton reportedly had a sister living nearby. While Swanton's marital status remains unclear, Bowman had been married and fathered a daughter, though her current location is unknown. Interestingly, neither man ever discussed their families. So many men and women during WWII had lost their families due to the hardship of war, the Dear John & Dear Jane letters being the worst. The two men became friends because of their backgrounds in flying boats and their sense of humor. Never a dull moment when around those two, together or individually!

According to Gardner, Swanton would save his money to come to the States several times a year. He would visit Mr. Wayne and other friends in California, and then, after meeting Haines, he would also come to Kansas.

Dillons traded the Beech "18" for a different model "18" as the company flagship in 1966, with the Gerbes grocery chain joining Dillons. The Beech 18 was replaced by a larger and faster Lockheed model 18, "Lodestar."

The Lockheed could accommodate up to 11 passengers compared to the Beech's 6. The L-18 was 30 MPH faster than the B-18. Dillon purchased the L-18 from an aircraft dealer at Dallas Love Field, Dallas, Texas. The dealer was Henry Seale, who had purchased several Phillips 66 Lodestars. Phillips had entered the jet age by purchasing Fanjet Falcon 20s, manufactured by Dassault Aviation of France, to replace the Lodestars. The Loadstar was large enough for a walk-around cabin and had an "almost" standup lavatory in the tail section. Its registration number was N666P.

Lockheed L-18 "Loadstar"
"Triple Six Papa" August 1966

At first, Ray Dillon Sr. didn't like the idea of the L-18 due to its passenger-carrying capacity. But Ace, Dick, and Haines convinced him of the advantages of speed and comfort the airplane provided. Ray relented, and the Board of Directors approved the acquisition.

Mr. Seale was a cool and calm character, and nothing seemed to rattle him. Haines was taking a demo flight with Henry in a different L-18 at Dallas's Love field when the left engine caught fire shortly after take-off! Haines thought, "Oh Crap"! Henry, almost nonchalantly according to Haines, called the control tower and said they needed to return for landing, not mentioning they had a fire. Henry then went through the fire and engine shutdown procedure without looking at the controls he used. They landed a few minutes later, and Henry told Haines, as if nothing had happened, "Let's take this one," referring to N666P.

Roy Gilbreath, who was working for Seale as a salesman/pilot at the time, related a story of Henry, himself, and a mechanic going to a small airport somewhere in Arkansas to pick up another L-18 that Henry had bought. The airplane had been sitting for some time and required a mechanic to look it over to determine if it was airworthy. They were ready to go after the inspection and a few minor repairs. As they boarded the airplane, the airport operator told them to back taxi on the runway as the taxiway was narrow and trees had recently been planted too close to it. Well, either Henry didn't hear the request, forgot it, or ignored it, so he went down the taxiway anyway. The wing tips of the old Lockheed were knocking small branches off the tender young trees!

But the real fun was just beginning. After takeoff, they retracted the landing gear, and the tail wheel would not retract. Several attempts were made with no success. Henry said a manual retract and extend mechanism was located next to the toilet in the lavatory at the rear of the cabin. Henry sent the mechanic back there to try and retract the tail wheel. He was back there for a while, and the tail wheel indicator still showed it in the down position. Henry then told Roy, "Go back there and see what's going on." Roy was back there for a while, crouched over the mechanic in an already cramped area struggling with the tail wheel when he felt someone's hot breath on the back of his neck! Who the hell's flying this thing? Both Roy and the mechanic ran over Henry to get to the cockpit. Fortunately, the auto pilot was functioning normally. The men experienced no harm, except perhaps for some soiled clothing. Needless to say, the tailwheel remained in the down position for the rest of the flight.

During this time, negotiations to have a central Missouri grocery company join Dillon Stores were underway. Negotiations were successful, and Gerbes Stores became a part of Dillon Stores.

Gerbes joins Dillon Stores.

Pictured are Ray Dillon Sr., far left, Ace Dillon, center, with hands crossed, and Dick Dillon, second from far right. Pictured between Ace and Dick are Mr. & Mrs. Gerbes. The remainder are executives of the Gerbes Stores Co.

The L-18 "Triple Six Papa" was not long in the fleet. Whether it was its cabin seating arrangement, its "Satanic" 666 in its "N" number, or for some other reason, it was traded for another L-18. This one had been modified by Bill Lear before he became occupied by his Biz-Jet Project. Modifications made by Lear led to increased speed and more cabin amenities, and it was now referred to as a "Learstar." Its "N" number was 153T.

"Learstar" 153 "Tango"

An embarrassing moment happened not long after 153T was in service. The plane was used for a trip to the old Kansas City airport. The airport only had one north-south runway. Haines was cleared to land to the north. Due to a taxiway closure, a miscommunication between air control and ground control in the control tower caused a Convair 340 airliner to back taxi on the runway to the south. Haines had already landed and was unable to make a go-around. The pilots of the Convair, trusting controllers, didn't see the Lockheed and proceeded to turn south on the runway, resulting in a nose-to-nose standoff! Fortunately, the Convair had Beta propellers and was able to back up! Haines was then able to turn the Lockheed around on the runway and end the dilemma.

As Haines became well known as an aircraft trader, many types of airplanes would come to Wells Aircraft as "For Sale or Trade" inventory. Ace would come out when something new and different came in, and he and Haines would have to "Test Hop" it, with Ace at the controls, of course!

One such airplane was the Cessna model 195. This airplane was Cessna's top-of-the-line in the late '40s and early '50s. With a cabin large enough for 5 Passengers and a cruise speed of 170 mph., it was the first Cessna to be called a "Business Liner." It was in the Dillon fleet for many years.

Bill Haines and the "195"

Another airplane was a Cessna model 336 "Skymaster," often affectionately referred to as the "Mixmaster." The 336 was a unique twin-engine airplane, with one engine located at the nose and the other at the rear of the fuselage; its sound in flight was instantly recognizable. The tail structure was supported by twin booms attached to the wings at each fuselage side.

Cessna 336 "Skymaster"
Photo courtesy of Chris England

It is unknown if the Dillons bought the 336 or simply used it. Either way, it was around for quite some time!

Later, Cessna replaced the model 336 with the model 337. It had a longer fuselage and retractable landing gear. Many variants were built, including a model with pressurization.

A model 337 aircraft was involved in an accident at Hutchinson. The plane was carrying members of the pilot/owner's family, who were to enjoy a sightseeing flight. The pilot/owner himself was visiting the family. Before takeoff, the rear engine refused to start. The Kansas wind was blowing quite strong out of the South that day. The pilot unwisely decided to go with just the front engine operating. The takeoff commenced off the south-oriented runway. The airplane became airborne, but the ascension was slow. Thinking that by retracting the landing gear, the rate of climb would increase, he made the mistake of doing so. The main gear doors hinged at the rear, and when they opened, they became huge airbrakes, pulling the airplane down! Fortunately, it had cleared the fence and road at the end of the runway and went down into an open field. The only harm done to passengers was perhaps the pilot's pride!

The airplane, however, was not so fortunate. Major damage occurred to the underside, landing gear, front-engine, and propeller. It took Wells Aircraft mechanics weeks to repair.

1968: The company changed its name from J.S. DILLON and Sons Stores to Dillon Companies Inc.

In late September 1968, Wanasek called his friend Mike Sims, whom Skycraft Inc. employed as a flight instructor and charter pilot, and asked if he would like a job flying twins. Sims replied, "Hell, yes! Who for?" Wanasek said he and Wells Aircraft were parting ways, and they would be looking for a replacement.

Wanasek and Sims had been lifelong friends. Their grandparents were neighbors in Hutchinson. Wanasek's mother and Sims's father had attended the same schools and grown up together. Steve Wanasek was one year older than Mike Sims, but they became close friends. Both were interested in flying. They often went for joy rides in Wanasek's Chief. They would fly under the high lines northwest of Hutchinson and buzz the local nudist colony. The colony was located in a grove of Catalpa trees which no longer exists. Of course, they did not see anything, but it sure sent some people scurrying for cover!

Sims interviewed for Wanasek's position, Haines flight-tested him, and Wells approved and hired him. Sims gave Skycraft his two weeks' notice and began working for Wells Aircraft on October 14, 1968.

January 1969: Dillon Co's Inc. goes on the New York Stock Exchange.

Near Disaster #3

In February 1969, Sims flew the company's attorney, Eugene White, to Topeka, Kansas. The trip was made in a Twin Beech that Haines had put in Well's inventory from Hood Airlines. Hood had used Beech 18s as commuter and feeder airliners in southern Texas. On the return flight nearing Hutchinson, Mr. White approached the cockpit and informed Sims that he smelled fuel fumes in the cabin. Sims stretched as far as he possibly could into the cabin without leaving the pilot's seat and confirmed fuel odor.

Wells's maintenance was informed, and they said they had found some rubber cross-feed fuel lines had deteriorated and replaced them. As with any maintenance involving operating systems, the airplane must be test-flown. Haines told Sims to go out and select cross-feed on the fuel valves and see if fumes were detected. Upon retracting the landing gear after takeoff, the landing gear circuit breaker popped. The gear up or unsafe red light was on, indicating the landing gear was up with the selector in the up position. Sims didn't reset it immediately, knowing that they had to cool down before resetting.

During the test flight using cross-feed, they found that fuel smells were worse than before. Well's maintenance was informed by radio of the situation with the fuel problem and the landing gear circuit breaker. They said, "Come back, and we'll fix it." Sims reset the circuit breaker and moved the landing gear selector to the down position. The gear down green light came on indicating safe to land. However, the gear circuit breaker promptly popped once more. As the Beech approached for landing, a Cessna 150 trainer was waiting for takeoff. As Sims touched down, the instructor pilot of the 150, Jim Little, started screaming, "Left gear, left gear!" As Sims sensed the airplane beginning to lean to the left, he immediately applied full power and aborted the landing. Miraculously, the left propeller did not strike the runway pavement!

Sims was scared for the first time in an airplane. In shock, he flew the aircraft away from the traffic pattern and began to breathe. Informing the control tower of his situation, he flew west of the city and contacted Wells via Unicom radio. Sims told Haines and Jim Hephner of the problematic situation. Along with Jay Frizzo, Mr. Carey's pilot, they consulted with Beechcraft engineers to troubleshoot the problem. The Beech engineers explained that the switches for the gear motor were on the left gear and the position light switches on the right. With the left gear inoperable, the right gear would bottom out, up or down, with the gear motor still powered, which caused the circuit breaker to pop.

After many failed attempts to lock down the left gear, it was decided to raise the right gear and make a belly landing. Due to the strong fuel odors, the crew contacted McConnell Air Force Base and asked if they could foam down a runway to prevent the possibility of fire. They replied that they could foam a taxiway for the landing.

Sims flew around for a while to burn off as much fuel as possible before landing. The belly landing was made smoothly with minimum damage.

Sims got quite a shock when opening the airstair door! Confronting him was an alien-looking creature pointing an alien-looking weapon at him! Of course, it was an Air Force fireman in a fireproof silver suit, and the weapon was a foam shooter!

Later that day, Little told Sims he noticed the left gear was not down as the Beech crossed the runway threshold. Little said he tried to get the microphone from his student to issue a warning, but in doing so in the excitement, he wound up juggling the microphone like a hot potato!

After Wells mechanics removed the upper cowlings and inspected the aircraft, they took these photos.

The next day, the crew lifted the plane and extended the landing gear. The left gear was "chained" in the down position. They then installed new propellers, and the plane flew back to Hutchinson the same day.

It was placed in a storage hanger while Haines and Hephner decided what to do with it. Eventually, they decided to restore it and make it a convertible between passenger and cargo.

In April 1969, Haines acquired an Aero Commander 680S. The S stood for supercharged. Being supercharged meant good performance at higher elevations. It was easy to fly, and Ace and Dick Dillon, along with other pilots, liked it. So it was added to the Dillon fleet. This began an era of Aero Commanders.

The first Dillon Aero Commander N6830S.

Ace, Dick, and Paul, along with their families, loved skiing, often flying into Aspen, Colorado. Although Paul was no longer flying as a pilot, he and his family would use it with Wells or Dillon pilots flying.

Commander 6830S was not certified for flight into known icing conditions. Haines found and put into Wells sales inventory a 680F. The F model was equipped with de-icing equipment, had radar, and was pressurized. It was still powered by the same engines as the S model, so performance was compromised. It was tried on some company trips and was found to be more costly to operate than the S model, so it was sold off.

6830S remained in the fleet until June of 1972. The company did not operate an Aero Commander again until August 1975. It was a model 690A. Turbo-Prop powered, had a larger cabin and was equipped for all-weather flight. It was in the fleet until October 1976.

Turbo Commander 690A

The firm determined that some passengers did not like the Aero Commanders as they were a bit claustrophobic. Sitting under the high wing and between the two engines bothered them.

The Turbo-Commander was a good performer but costly to operate.

In May 1969, Haines got a request from Gardener for a P-51 "Mustang." Fortunately, Haines found one close by in Enid, Oklahoma. The Champlin Oil Company family owned it. He bought it for $50,000.00. (to buy a flying example today would cost in the 7-figure range!)

The selling price, or the commission to Wells, was never disclosed.

The Champlain P-51D

Upon finalizing the deal, Bowman was tasked with flying the plane to Oakland, California. There, it was to have the rear seat removed and a ferry tank installed by Vic Coss of Coss Aircraft Tanking Service. Not long into the flight, Bowman noticed the engine temperature rising. The '51s Rolls Royce "Merlin" engine is liquid-cooled and has two coolant pumps, one of which had failed. Bowman landed at Borger, TX., and notified Hephner of the problem. Hephner, also a pilot, found a replacement pump, and he and another mechanic flew to Borger and fixed the problem.

As Bowman was preparing to continue the flight, a young lineman asked him if he would put on an "Airshow" when he left. Bowman replied: "Young man, every time I take off in this damned thing, it's an airshow"!

In June 1969, Dick Dillon earned his instrument rating.

During this time, Dillon Co. Inc. negotiated mergers with City Markets of Grand Junction, Colorado, and Quik Stops convenience stores in northern California. The negotiations with City Markets were successful, and they joined Dillon Co's Inc. in 1969.

The addition of City Markets and the potential acquisition of Quik Stops required flights across the Continental Divide. For safety and comfort, this needed a pressurized airplane.

Also, negotiations were being made to acquire Fry's Super Markets in Arizona and California. With visions of the future, pressurization plus long range were considered in replacing the Learstar. Speed, passenger comfort, cost, pressurization, and range were required.

The selection was narrowed to the Grumman Gulfstream I or the Howard 500. Both were nearly equal in size and speed. The Gulfstream was turbine-powered, and radial reciprocating engines powered the 500.

Grumman Gulfstream 1
Photo by Bill Larkins 🗗#4

The cost of the Grumman was twice the price of the Howard, and with Aircraft Engine Service a Dillon subsidiary, the 500 won hands down!

With the acquisition of the Howard, the Learstar was sold off. However, in the early '70s, it made a return to Hutchinson, albeit not literally but figuratively, as in a movie. At the time, there was a drive-in theater just southeast of the airport, nearly in line with the approach to runway 31. Sims and his wife went to the drive-in one evening and, by chance, parked next to Rick Lorenz and his wife. Rick was one of Wells Aircraft's lead mechanics. The movie being shown was very risqué but not X-rated. In one scene, some people are awaiting the arrival of the movie's star actress at an airport. And there it was, the still green and white Learstar 153T. Shown on approach, landing, and pulling up to the waiting crowd. Stunned and amused at the same time, the Sims and Lorenz's were amazed to see their old airplane in a soft porn movie!

The Dillon Co's Howard 500-N277X

The Howard 500 was very similar in appearance to the Loadstar because it incorporated components of the Lockheed breed. But the Howard 500 was a new airplane. It was certified in the "Airline Transport" Category under then FAR 04B.

Durrell "Dee" Unger Howard established the Howard Aero Company in 1947 in San Antonio, Texas. His first employee was another aircraft engineer, Ed Swearingen, who later formed his own aircraft company.

The concept of the 500 came from a wealthy Mexican oil producer in 1957 who wanted an airplane that would fly from Mexico City to New York City. It would have to be fast and roomy for such a long flight. Howard had been converting WWII aircraft, primarily surplus Lockheed airplanes, for some time. The L-18 Loadstar became the Howard Model 250. The PV-1 Ventura became the Howard 350. But neither of these had the speed or range required.

Other aircraft companies were modifying surplus military aircraft—primarily the North American B-25 and the Douglas B-26.

One such company was located at the Hutchinson Municipal Airport by Rock Island Oil & Refining Co., a subsidiary of Koch Industries of Wichita, KS. They bought a dozen or more surplus B-26s, converting them for corporate transport. The finished product was called the Monarch 26. How many were converted is unknown, but Koch operated two of them in their corporate fleet located in Hutchinson.

The Monarch 26

Fred Koch was a friend of Bill Lear's, and during the certification of his jet to fly into known icing conditions, one of the B-26s was made into an icing machine. Quite an engineering marvel, it incorporated a water tank in the fuselage, a retractable ladder-like apparatus with variable nozzle openings to produce different types of icing conditions. The ladder was designed to keep the jet out of the B-26's wake. It was tricky to operate and fly due to the drag it produced. It is the only one known to exist at the time.

The Monarch 26 "Ice Machine".

While the Corporate Jet age was blossoming in the '60s, sales of the various bomber conversions waned, and Rock Island ceased modifications of the B-26. With the certification of the Lear Jet, Koch sold off its two Monarch 26s and began operating Lear Jets in 1969.

Haines and Wells Aircraft took one under consignment. Haines and Gardner sold it, and it went to somewhere in Malaysia.

Consigned Monarch 26

None of these other conversions met the requirements of Howard's customer.

So, the engineering wheels in Dee's head began turning. His idea was to make a new fuselage that was pressurized and longer than the Ventura, a new wing carrying more fuel and larger engines providing more speed and performance.

Howard 500 fuselage jig
Photo Courtesy of Dee Howard International Education Foundation. (DHEDF)

This new jig provides fuselage bulkheads to be placed 6 inches apart for pressurization. It is also 4 feet longer than the Ventura.

The 500-wing jig
Photo Courtesy of DHEDF

Howard bought the Ventura outer wing jigs from Lockheed and modified them to make the wings "wet" to carry more fuel. A wet wing is now the fuel tank instead of individual tanks or cells. The significant modification was incorporating Fowler-type wing flaps, which increased the wing area when extended.

The center section of the wing structure came from the Lockheed PV-2 "Harpoon," which is heavier than the Ventura. This is to accommodate the heavier weight of the 500 and the power of the Pratt & Whitney R-2800 engines.

Mounting the P & W R-2800 CB16/17
Photo Courtesy of DHEDF

The R-2800, as a CB-17, could produce 2500 horsepower using 145 octane fuel and an anti-detonation injection (ADI) fluid comprised of alcohol and water. It is white in color and referred to as "Mouse Milk." Detonation means premature ignition of the fuel/air mixture in the cylinders, which could cause engine failure. If ADI were unavailable, they operated as CB-16s with reduced power settings and performance.

Howard Aero Incorporated manufactured only 23 of the Howard 500, the most sophisticated piston engine-powered business aircraft ever built. Notably, 22 were sold, with Howard retaining the prototype for himself.

The sophisticated systems that were in the 500's

An engine-driven supercharger on the left engine supplies cabin pressurization. This provided a cabin altitude of 4,500 feet at an altitude of 25,00 feet. Pressurization was not found on piston-powered business airplanes of this era.

Two-speed superchargers on the engines for high-altitude performance

Auto disengage of the cabin supercharger if the right engine were to fail because the supercharger robbed the left engine of some power. Critical in emergencies.

Propeller auto feather on a failed engine.

Rudder boost in the event of an engine failure to assist in maintaining directional control.

Yaw limiter.

Engine analyzer. If an engine began to run rough, the crew could determine the cause of the problem. The R-2800's had 18 cylinders and 36 spark plugs. If a cylinder or spark plug failed, the crew could determine which it was.

AC electrical system for windshield heat and gally cook stove.

And for the ladies, a lavatory with vanity and flushing toilet!

Stella Dillon, Ray's wife, particularly loved this feature.

The 500 was featured in many articles by aviation publications such as Aviation History, AOPA Pilot and Flying Magazine.

The Dillons 500, N277X, even made the cover of Flying Magazine in October of 1993. Its owner at the time is unknown but believed to have been Timken Roller Bearing Co. of Rochester, NY. The cover photo and the portrait photo featured in the article were taken by photographer 'George Larson' in 1976. The airplane received a repaint between 1973 and 1976.

Ace commissioned a large portrait of the airplane in flight from Flying Magazine's photo of it from the article. This portrait hung in the lobby of Wells Aircraft until Wells was sold to Don Rogers, Well's current owner. It now adorns Sims's "Man cave."

The original portrait was severely faded by the florescent lighting in Well's lobby. Sims had it reduced in size vertically and the colors restored professionally. The original is behind the restored portrait.

The last flying example, owned by Tony Phillippi of Phillippi Equipment Co., was awarded Grand Champion of the EAA's Air Venture convention held at Oshkosh, Wisconsin, in 1997.

The airplane is truly unique. "If you want to make the latest and greatest of the Gulfstream Biz. Jets just disappear," Phillippi was heard to say, "pull up on the ramp next to it with the Howard 500!"

Interior similar to the Dillon 500. View looking aft. The Dillon's 500 interior was made in plush leather. Photo Courtesy of DHEDF.

The typical interior of the 500 was 12 occupants.
A crew of two.

Cockpit jump seat.

Main cabin 9-Passenger.

3 place couch & 6 place club seating with stowaway tables.

The main cabin was 6'2" tall and 27' long.

For a piston-powered airplane, the 500 was very smooth and quiet. The huge props turned at less than half the revolutions of the engines. The gear ratio was .45 to 1.

Contrary to some accounts, the 500 was easy to fly. Once the pilot learned its characteristics, take-offs and landings became routine.

During training to fly the 500, Haines asked Ace if Sims could also be type-rated. Ace wisely said, "NO!" Sims had been with the Company for less than a year." This rating would give him credentials to find another job at our expense."

At this time, the first Apollo Moon landing was to take place. While Haines was pouring over the many performance charts for the 500, Sims had acquired a six-pack of beer. Sitting on the end of his bed in the hotel, watching the moon landing while drinking beer, he cried like a baby when Armstrong took that historic first step!

Photograph taken in Peterborough, Ontario, Canada, August 1969.

The airport had just opened in 1969. In 2019, this photo is believed to have been displayed at ceremonies commemorating the 50th anniversary of its opening.

The following stampings were made on the backside of this photograph.

Winner of the Ernie Bourne Memorial Trophy awarded by the Professional Photographers of Ontario for the best Commercial Photograph in Colour

This picture is copyrighted and must not be copied or allowed to be copied or communicated to anyone else without written permission by
PETERBOROUGH AIRWAYS LIMITED
705 745 - 7370   .OX 417
PETERBOROUGH, ONT, CANADA
SERIAL NUMBER   691486

Ray Dillon, in gray suit; First Officer Sims, and, in the cockpit, Captain Haines.

Ray Dillon was taking his son Dick and his three sons on a fishing trip at Barney Lamb's "Ball Lake Lodge," located north of Kenora, accessible only by seaplane. Haines and Sims got to go along to stay at the lodge and fish.

Lamb had a Twin Beech on floats with an emergency escape hatch over the cockpit. Haines had never seen one and inquired of its origin. Lamb said it was only certified in Canada but was available in kit form. Being as "ornery" as Haines was, thinking of the Beech that Sims had bellied in, he asked Lamb if he could get one before we left for home. Lamb was able to, and Haines "smuggled" it into the States in the aft belly baggage compartment of the 500!

Not only was Dillon Co's Inc. expanding, but so was its subsidiary, Wells Aircraft Inc. Haines had been negotiating with Skycraft Inc. about a proposed buyout. The parties came to terms, and the Hutchinson City Commission approved the deal on November 1, 1969.

From the Hutchinson News November 1, 1969.

Wells Buying Skycraft

Wells Aircraft Inc. is purchasing the major assets of SkyCraft Inc., it was announced Tuesday afternoon.

According to Robert Armstrong, SkyCraft president, and William F. Haines, vice president of Wells, the sale becomes effective Nov. 1.

Explaining the sale, Armstrong declared, "Due to the demands of my other business interests here in Hutchinson and in Western Kansas, I've been considering this move for some time."

Armstrong has operated SkyCraft for the past nine years.

Haines added, "With the combined operations, we will have 20 employes, 10 of whom are aircraft mechanics. With the increasing demand for aircraft service and repair, we will probably have double that number a year from now."

Haines said Wells will "continue all present services. We also intend to offer additional services such as multi-engine charter service and multi-engine cargo service for the western half of Kansas."

The new operation will be known as Wells Aircraft and the SkyCraft name will be discontinued.

City Roundup

Okay Lease Transfer

A two-page agenda proved to be routine for city commissioners Tuesday. They completed the agenda in less than one hour.

They: Declared Oct. 12 "Columbus Day" honoring, according to the proclamation signed by Mayor Ken Keast, "the most spectacular discovery" — Christopher Columbus' discovery of the New World:

Approved the transfer of Skycraft's lease to Wells Aircraft Co. Wells is purchasing Skycraft. Also approved Wells' lease of a hangar at the airport for $115 a month. The hangar was previously leased by Security Elevator Co.

Lease Approved

With the acquisition of Sky craft, Mr. Carey's pilot, Jay Frizzo who was of Italian desent, did not wish to be a part of the management of the new venture. Frizzo had become friends with Tenneco's chief pilot, Tony Zuma, who was also of Italian descent. Nearing retirement age, Frizzo wanted to fly jets before retirement. Tenneco was operating a variety of turbine aircraft, including a Vickers Viscount four-engine turboprop, a Fairchild F-27 turboprop, and two or more Dassault Fan Jet Falcons. Zuma assured Frizzo he would find a position for him if Mr. Carey had no objections to Frizzo moving to Tenneco.

Frizzo informed Mr. Carey of his wishes to fly turbines and no longer be a part of Wells Aircraft. Mr. Carey was understanding and wished Frizzo the best in his new venture. He and Ray Dillon Sr. then sold their shares of Wells to Dillon Real Estate Division. Wells Aircraft then became a wholly owned subsidiary of Dillon Co's. Inc.

Frizzo flew for Tenneco for several years, being based in Racine, WI, and Bakersfield, CA.

Jay was a genius at reading primitive airborne radar. In the spring of 1969, Jay and Sims, as co-pilot, were to depart McAllen, TX., for Houston. There was a building line of thunderstorms along the route, and Jay told Sims to fly, and he would work the radar. *En route*, Jay would ask Air Traffic Control (ATC) for deviations around cells of the storms. As they worked through the storms, a commercial flight from the west asked ATC, "Where the hell is that Beech 18, and how high is he? We can't find a hole anywhere!"

Bob Bowman was now assigned to be Mr. Carey's pilot as a contractor for Wells. Bowman was now paid per diem by Wells Aircraft and not on salary to Carey.

Chapter Four: The 1970s Soaring Times!

The '1970s began with the Skycraft hangars re-model. Both were equal in square footage, but the north hangar (#1) was much taller than the south (#2). The two were joined on the ramp side by a small lobby and a parts room with a customer counter on the backside of the lobby. A small office for the service manager was on the south side of the parts room, and men's and ladies' bathrooms were on the north side. There was an open space between the two hangars behind the parts room.

Haines, Hephner, and office manager Darrel Luman planned an expansion to the rear of the existing parts room. It would include an expanded lobby receptionist's area behind the relocated counter. New offices for the Vice President and General manager (Haines), office manager (Luman), and service manager (Hephner). A new pilot office, combination class/conference room, a storage room for office supplies, an avionics shop, an employee break room, an employee bathroom, a machine shop, a larger parts room, and a storage area for bulk liquid supplies.

Wells Aircraft also planned an expansion of the Security Grain hanger (#3) located just south of the old Skycraft hangars. The development was to the rear of the building to house the Dillon Co.'s Inc. airplanes.

Also in the planning stage was a new storage hangar (#4) located between Sparks Aviation and the old Wells Aircraft hangar (#5).

After approval by the Dillon Co.'s Inc. board, Ace (Ace was President of Wells for corporate reasons), and the City of Hutchinson, construction contracts were awarded. The City Parks division operates the Hutchinson Municipal Airport, and all structures are owned by the city and leased to the occupants.

Hangars were now numbered by leases to Wells by the city. Number one was the large hangar on the north and consecutively to the south to hangar number 5, the old Wells hangar.

Operations during construction were hectic at best, but the assimilation of Skycraft employees went smoothly. Sims was placed in charge of the flight school and charter departments. At the time, only Jim Little transitioned from Skycraft as a flight instructor and charter pilot. Skycraft had established an FAA-approved flight school under FAR Part 141. Wells soon expanded the school, adding more instructors and charter pilots to the staff. This allowed the school to accommodate more students and offer a wider variety of courses.

The first were Roger Humiston, Randy Stapleton, Mike Green, Merlin "Skip" Mills of Hutchinson, and Gene Kubin of McPherson, KS.

Humiston wasn't sure of his position after an incident with Haines's mother and daughter. He was to fly the two ladies to Vichy, Mo., in one of the Mooney's. Approaching the destination, Roger saw what he thought was the Vichy airport and proceeded to land. Turning off the runway, the airplane was quickly surrounded by military police! Surprised and scared at the same time, they learned that they had landed at Fort Leonard Wood Army airfield. After explaining the mistake, the base commander allowed them to continue their trip without repercussions. Haines, fortunately for Humiston, found the event quite amusing but didn't let Humiston know that!

Twin Beech 123EM was put in the shop hangar (#2) when remodeling was complete. It spent the next two years being rebuilt as a convertible. It could be configured to carry up to 8 passengers or become a cargo carrier with the seats removed. It had a combination airstair/cargo door. Remember the escape hatch Haines smuggled in? Hephner installed the kit, he and the Canadian manufacturer applied for a US Standard Type Certificate for it and got approval from the FAA. Now, the Canadian Co. could sell the kit in the US.

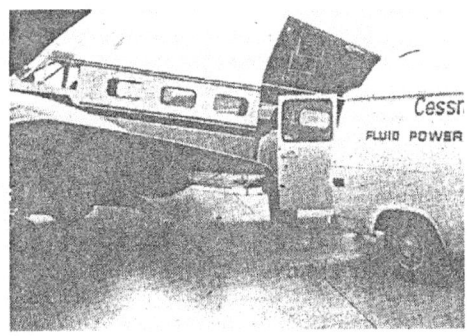

The only photos found by the author of 123EM after rebuilding.

It was the queen of Wells Aircraft charter planes, serving the public and the Dillon Co's. It remained in service well into the late 1970s.

Negotiations with Quik Stops convenience stores were successful, and they joined Dillon Co. Inc. in 1970.

Jim Hephner earns his Instrument rating.

In 1971, at the Supermarket Association's annual convention in New York City, Dillon Co's Inc. was in the Howard 500. Also, Kroger Co. was in its Grumman Gulfstream 1. Both airplanes were located in Teterboro, NJ's General Aviation Airport.

At departure time, the Kroger plane was just in front of the Dillon plane. The Kroger plane was cleared for takeoff just a few minutes before Dillon's N27X in November of that year

Both airplanes flew the same route, resulting in ATC handoffs occurring on the same frequencies. Initially, ???K received the first few handoffs. However, during the transition from NY ATC Center to Chicago Center, ATC handed off to Nov. 277X first, followed by ???K. At this point, the Howard had passed the Grumman.

The Grumman was flying higher than the Howard and possibly into stronger headwinds. Did Dillons or Haines care? No, the Howard had outrun the G-1!

Hephner to the rescue!

Sometime in the 1970's, an emergency arises in Hutchinson's airspace. A man and his wife are to land at Hutchinson Municipal Airport in a twin-engine Aero Commander. During their approach, the husband/ pilot becomes incapacitated! The wife is not a pilot and scared but has courage enough to pick up the radio mike and tell the control tower what has happened. One of the controllers is a pilot and is able to instruct her in how to circle southwest of the airport while they find a pilot familiar with the Aero Commander. It is a Saturday or Sunday and the time before cell phones. Mr. Haines cannot be reached; Sims is playing golf and is out of touch. Hephner is third on the towers call list and the only pilot the control tower is able to contact! Despite never being a flight instructor, Jim is cool and calmly able to talk the lady to a successful landing! He has the praise and admiration of all those who know him!

Hollywood returns to Hutchinson.

In the mid 1950's, the movie "Picnic" was filmed in Hutchinson and The cities of Nickerson, Halstead and others. Then in the spring of 1972, production began on the movie "Ace Eli and Rodger of the Skies." The flight crew and airplanes are based at Wells Aircraft and flight scenes filmed at various locations around Hutchinson. It is the story of a WWI widowed pilot barnstorming in the 1920s and his young son Rodger. An adventure-comedy film centered around Eli and 11-year-old Rodger. Wherever they go, Eli finds a new girlfriend. He favors one, Shelby, but does not form a permanent relationship. When Shelby leaves Eli, Rodger is saddened and, at one time, even hires a prostitute to Comfort his father.

The film starred:	Cliff Robertson (a pilot in real life) as Eli
	Pamela Franklin as Shelby
	Eric Shea as Rodger
	Bernadette Peters (movie debut) as Allison
Supporting cast:	Rosemary Murphy as Hannah
	Alice Ghostly as Sister Lite
	Royal Dano as Jake

"ACE ELI AND RODGER OF THE SKIES' © 1973 20th Century Studios, Inc. All rights reserved."

The company contracted to do the flight scenes arrived in the late spring of 1972. They trucked in two Curtis JN-4D "Jenny's." The Jenny is almost synonymous with American aviation in the 1920s. The Jenny was a WWI primary trainer, but its more significant role in aviation history was as a barnstorming and mail-carrying airplane.

The Curtiss JN-4D "Jenny"
Photo by Bill Larkins ⌕ #5

The aviation company contracted was headed by a well-known Hollywood pilot who had flown scenes in many movies.

Harry Swanton happened to come to Hutchinson as filming was to begin. He told Haines, "I know this guy; he's logged more time sitting in a wrecked airplane waiting for an ambulance than he's logged in flight!"

Out of respect and privacy, he will be called "Jack."

Despite Swanton's scathing remark, Jack was a charming and likable fellow. He often regaled the younger pilots of the area who were fortunate enough to meet him.

Having been a barnstormer, Roland Wells was, of course, interested in the goings on. While admiring the Jenny, he said to the mechanic in charge and Haines that "Jack should be careful of the Kansas winds as they can come up unexpectedly and if ignored could lead to a 'Crack-Up' because these Jenny's are like a big kite and vulnerable to the wind."

The flight scenes were to be filmed over wheat and hay fields just west of Mount Hope, which was renamed "Monument" for the movie. The only contribution of Wells Aircraft to the movie was the use of the Dillon Co's hangar for the care of the Jenny's. One of Wells's pilots flew a movie extra who dropped leaflets over "Monument" announcing the arrival of Barnstormer Eli. Of course, all you saw in the movie were the leaflets falling over "Monument."

And sure enough, as Roland Wells had cautioned, it happened. While performing a low-level fly-by of a crowd of movie extra spectators, he was flying downwind, approaching a row of trees rapidly and trying to turn sharply, being low, he contacted the ground with a wing and pancaked the Jenny to the ground. The landing gear was torn out from under the Jenny and caused other minor damage. Fortunately, there were no injuries to him or his star passenger, Pamela Franklin!

Also, in early '72', Haines acquired a Douglas DC-3 for sale to Gardener. Gardener had a customer looking for an airplane that could carry more than just a few passengers, and the DC-3 fit the bill. It was still configured as an airliner with 20+ seats.

Douglas DC-3
Photo courtesy of Chris England

Haines bought the "3" from aircraft dealer Jack Adams of "Two Jacks Aircraft Sales" of Little Rock, AK. The "Two Jacks" name was for Jack Sr., and Jack Jr. Adams Sr. was well known in large airplane sales and as a showman. His operations base was adorned outside with a display of two large "Jax" replicas and an equally large "Jax Ball."

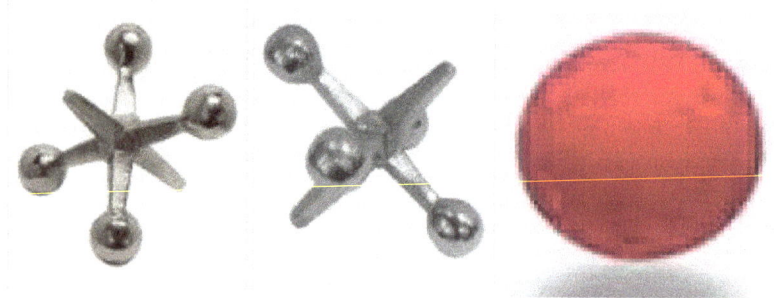

Inside the customer lobby was a huge rocking chair for photo ops with customers and/or their families seated.

Haines flew the "3" from Little Rock to Hutchinson on a ferry permit as he was not rated to fly it. Type ratings are required to fly airplanes with a gross weight of 12,500 lbs. or more or are turbojet-powered. The DC-3 grosses at 26,900 lbs.

Haines so enjoyed flying the "3" that he talked Gardener into letting him get his type rating.

Ace permitted Haines to deal in DC-3s with the rating in hand. He would sometimes take Hephner with him to look over a "3" before purchase, and if bought, the two would fly it home. But neither Haines nor Hephner was often available due to Dillon's or Wells's responsibilities. Haines would have to contract a crew to fly a prospective purchase to Hutchinson for inspection. This was often expensive.

Swanton was rated in the "3," and when he was in town, Haines would send him to fly them to Wells when he was tied up. On the first occasion, Haines sent Swanton and a young Wells pilot, Randy Stapleton, to somewhere in New York to fly one to Hutchinson. Stapleton was flabbergasted to learn Swanton didn't know how to file a US flight plan or navigate with the VOR Navigation System or Victor Airways. Swanton had flown in that part of the world still using low-frequency "range" navigation systems. Stapleton did the flight planning and filing for their adventure and taught Swanton to navigate with the nav, which was new to him. The young Stapleton enjoyed the experience with the "old salt" Swanton!

In the meantime, Sims had been pestering Haines to let him get rated in the "3" for quite a while! Sims has wanted to fly the "3s" since childhood. When Sims was just a young boy, he would ride his bicycle to the airport and watch the planes come and go. Those he liked the most were the Beech 18 and the DC-3. Wanting to be a pilot when he grew up, those two planes plus the Boeing B-17 (of "Twelve o'clock High" movie fame) were the ones he wanted to fly the most!

Sims was already flying the '18" and was joyously rated in the "3" in Oct. of "72". It seemed the B-17 would evade him.

The large and the small.

Haines bought a 152 Cessna trainer and converted it to a "Texas Taildragger" to train pilots in the operation of conventional gear airplanes.

Haines bought and sold many DC-3s during the '70s. Putting one on Wells charter service was considered but deemed too regulatory and costly. When piloted by Dillon pilots, Haines or Sims, Dillon Co's Inc. could use them and did so on a few occasions.

1972 was a busy year. Company management recognized that an airplane in Grand Junction for City Markets would increase the efficiency of operations there. City Market stores were located in mountainous areas where travel by automobile from one location to another was time-consuming. Not only to executive personnel but to store services if something in a store fails. For example, a refrigeration unit.

At Ace and Dicks direction, Haines placed a Cessna 402 there and hired a local former Navy pilot to fly and care for it.

Cessna 402

Photo by Ahunt at en Wikipedia (Original reg.# C-FFAP) ⓢ

The 402 was a cabin class, turbo-charged but unpressurized, twin-engine plane. It performed well in the mountains with turbocharged twin engines.

Also, in early 1972, Fry's Food Stores of Arizona and northern California joined Dillon Co's Inc. This, along with the Quik Stops convenience stores located in the San Francisco Bay Area, also called for more frequent flights to that area.

The former Naval pilot of City Markets moved on to other things in 1974, and another local pilot was hired. That pilot was a young man named Lincoln Hall. Hall was a native of Grand Junction and knew mountain flying. He would serve City Markets and Dillon Co's Inc. for many years.

With the addition of Fry's and Quik Stops, Ace petitioned the Board of Directors to approve the purchase of a jet airplane. The jet would make it possible to make the trip to California and back to Hutchinson in one day.

In May, the Directors approved the purchase with a limit of one million dollars. Several Corp. jets were available, but only three had price tags of less than a million. They were: The newly certified Cessna 500 "Citation," the Lear Jet model "25," and the North American/Rockwell model 40A "Sabreliner."

Cessna 500 "Citation"
Photo by Rob Hodgkins ☐ #6

The Citation 500 was eliminated from contention early on. It was only about 75 miles per hour faster than the Howard 500 and didn't have enough range to make California non-stop. An in-route fuel stop would be required, thus negating the slight increase in speed over the Howard.

Cessna's marketing campaign was quite aggressive. Full-page promotional ads were placed in all the Aviation Trade magazines. They touted the competitors as being "Fuel Guzzling Luxury Barges." They even made model fuel trucks to illustrate the difference in fuel consumption between them and their competitors.

But the Citation was ridiculed in some circles. It was called the "Slowtation" and other disparaging terms.

The Citation evolved into a bigger, faster, and longer-ranged airplane. It eventually outsold all the other bizjets of its class combined! Cessna continued developing its Bizjet line and is competing with the "Big Boys" today!

Lear Jet "25"
Photo courtesy of Roger Humiston

The Learjet was close to home, being built in Wichita, so it was contacted for a demonstration flight. They sent a sales crew with a demo 25 for the flight. They showed the cabin and its amenities, then did a walk around the exterior, pointing out features of its structure.

Then, when entering the airplane to show the cockpit, they didn't ask Haines to sit in it! One climbed into the pilot seat while the other closed the cabin door and climbed into the co-pilot seat.

After briefly explaining the control systems' locations and functions, the engines were started, and the plane was taxied out for takeoff. Haines knelt behind the pilots as they meticulously went through the pre-takeoff checklist. Once completed, Haines and Sims were buckled in for takeoff back in the cabin.

Once in flight, Haines was never asked to take control of the Learjet!

It was later revealed that the Lear 25 had terrible stall characteristics!

Back on the ground, Haines told Sims, there are a lot of go-no-go systems. The airplane had to have two autopilots, two yaw dampers, a stick pusher if nearing a high altitude stall, a stick puller if going too fast and could not be hand flown above twenty-some thousand feet.

The decision was made to have a demo flight in the Sabreliner.

Sabreliner "40A"

North American/Rockwell (NAR) sent a demo plane crew with a lot of experience and confidence in the Sabre. The captain and demo pilot was a retired Air Force Colonel, Glenn Crumm. Crumm had flown the Sabre in its military form, the T-29, for years.

After the amenities and features were shown, Crumm had Haines take the pilot seat and talk him through the engine start, taxi, and take-off procedures. Crumm seldom touched the controls through the entire flight, including landing. He had Haines do it all!

They went to a safe altitude during the flight, and Crumm had Haines do some basic maneuvers. Then Crumm talked Haines through a "Barrel Roll"! It began with a 30-degree banked clearing turn with the airplane trimmed and power set to maintain altitude at 250 knots indicated. Then the aircraft was leveled, letting the trim bring the nose pitch up to 20 degrees. Then, the aileron control was deflected by ½, left or right, and held through the roll until the wings were level again. It went very smoothly.

Sims was seated in the cabin with the other demo pilot, the sales representative for NAR. He was telling Sims about how well the Sabre flew and how reliable it was as Haines was flying. At one time, Sims noticed something out the window and saw the ground was where the sky should be! "Oh, "&*#%" Sims thought, what's going on? Had he not looked out during the roll, he might never have known it happened!

After landing, Crumm put Sims in the pilot seat and repeated the entire routine.

Ace was informed of the demonstration and came to look the Sabre over. Crumm invited Ace to go for a flight, but Ace declined for some reason.

Ace, Haines, and the two NAR pilots discussed the differences between the Lear and the Sabre. Haines recommended the Sabre, and Ace agreed. Ace then signed the purchase agreement for a new Sabreliner 40A with a delivery date of mid-February 1973.

The smiles on Haines's and Sims's faces lasted for days!

Sims had not yet obtained his Airline Transport Pilot (ATP) rating, and Haines informed him that he would have to have one to be typed in the Sabre for insurance purposes. Sims immediately worked on it and obtained it in the restored Twin Beech 123EM.

The purchase agreement included ground school to learn the operational systems of the Sabreliner for two pilots. The course lasted for a week, and Haines could not escape his duties at Wells and Dillons. Planning to have Bowman, as a long-time contractor with Wells and Dillons, as his main go-to as a co-pilot on the Sabre, Haines scheduled him and Sims to go to the school in November.

With the purchase of the Sabre over the Citation, Ray Dillon Sr. was asked to leave the Cessna Board of Directors.

In the early seventies, two new instructor/charter pilots were hired to join Little, Humiston, and Stapleton in the Wells Aircraft Flight Dept. Kubin had moved on to bigger and better things. The two new hires are Brian Friesen and Bryce Reichert.

Near disaster strikes again involving 123EM. Bowman and Friesen are on a charter to Minneapolis, MN, when the right gear fails. This time, though, the crew was aware of the failure. A gear-up landing was made on an unused taxiway, with no foam this time, again with minor damage and no injuries.

As Bowman was shutting things down, he noticed the escape hatch over the cockpit was open. Bowman immediately thought, well, that damned kid (Friesen) has already bailed out! But, as he turned to exit the cockpit, Bowman saw Friesen was already tending to the scared and upset passengers!

Friesen and 123EM, it seemed, just didn't get along. Now, as captain, on a charter to Memphis, TN. He encountered severe turbulence over northern Arkansas when carrying two overhauled GE engines out of Strother Field of Winfield/Ark City, KS. The turbulence caused one or both GE engines to dislodge from their moorings, causing the cabin escape hatch to come loose and depart the airplane. The airplane was inverted at one point, and a miracle the old Beech didn't come apart! The GE engines were unloaded after landing safely at the destination. Friesen flew the airplane back to Hutchinson minus the cabin escape hatch.

The hatch was found in the middle of Main Street in Ft. Smith, AR. Some weeks passed when the FAA arrived at Hephner's office with it and inquired if it belonged to 123EM. The airplane was located just outside Hephner's office window with an escape hatch on it. Hephner pointed to it, and the FAA remarked that it looked like the one we found. Hephner replied, "That's a pretty common color, isn't it"? The feds just looked at each other, shook their heads, and walked out the door!

Wells Aircraft Inc. is now well established in the mid 1970s. The following photos are representative of the success achieved by Haines and Hephner.

**Wells Aircraft Lobby, circa 1995
(Note the Howard 500 portrait on the back wall).**

Hangar 1

Service Manager Jim Hephner is seated on the stairs. From L to R: Ralph Green, Bob Tracey, Chuck Montgomery, Ed Willis, and Dean Wedman.

Avionics technician George Clobes and his wife Karalee "Kay."

General aviation was booming in the '70s, and Haines bought and sold many airplanes.

In addition to Mr. Adams, Haines was doing business with a Denver, CO, dealer named Talmage "Tal" Miller. Miller was another WWII vet and a very entertaining character. He would often imitate President Franklin Roosevelt's mannerisms and speech.

Another was a young, handsome, and articulate guy named Jan Mann. Mann was based out of Phoenix, AZ. He had an uncanny resemblance to actor Michael Landon and the ability to charm the flies off a garbage truck!

Also, there was a fellow in Wichita, KS., Jimmy Alexander, who worked with Haines in sales of a local nature. He was diplomatic in resolving issues with a customer and the condition of an airplane for sale.

All of these sales companies became good customers of Wells Aircraft. If a customer wanted a pre-purchase inspection done, they would bring the airplane to Wells for the inspection. And, at times, their customers came along to get acquainted with Wells and witness the inspection. Many were impressed with Wells's work and returned their planes to Wells for routine maintenance.

Haines buys Twin Beech H18 - N177X. It is believed to be Olive Ann Beech's personal airplane before going to the turboprop Beech "King Air." It is put into the Dillon fleet.

Tri-gear Twin Beech H-18
Photo by Aeroprints.com #7

The H-18 Twin Beech was available in a tri-gear version of the venerable "18", making it easier to handle on the ground. The gross weight was increased to accommodate the added weight of the nose gear, and thus performance deteriorated a little. It was the last iteration of the 18 from the factory. Other variations of it were modifications by different companies.

The N-numbers 177X, 277X and 477X were now or once owned by Dillon Co's. Inc. Although 377X was not on the Dillon Co's Inc. fleet roster, it was owned briefly by Wells. It was a Howard 350 that Haines sold to Gardener to go to a company in Singapore. Gardener reported sometime later that the crew overshot a runway on landing, and the airplane wound up destroyed in a rice paddy!

A Cessna model 340 was also added to the fleet sometime in the early 70's.

Cessna 340
Photo courtesy of Acroterion ⌕ **#8**

The 340, although similar in appearance to the 400 series, was much smaller. It was a derivative of the 310/320, using their wing, tail, engine, and fuel system. The fuselage, however, was of the cabin type and pressurized.

The N number on it was N5004Q. When communicating with Air Traffic Control, the proper phonetic identification method is twin Cessna five zero zero four Quebec. Then, when acknowledging their instructions, the reply would be zero four Quebec. But some pilots would reply to a controller, one they knew had a good sense of humor, as "Oh four que"!

It served in the fleet for a few years.

Back in the day, smoking was still socially accepted, and its hazards to health were not fully known. By emptying the ashtrays, the line service personnel always knew who was flying and who was the first officer. In doing so, they would look at the butts and know who it was.

Haines: Viceroy

Sims: Marlboro Lights

Bowman: Winston

Hephner: Kool's

Powell: Smoked a pipe, but not while flying.

Powel was afflicted with a common ailment in seniors. Known as "Essential Tremors," it caused shaky hand movements but didn't affect his flying ability. Often, when trying to smoke his pipe, he had to steady the pipe stem with one finger of one hand while using the other to get it into his mouth.

One day, Powel was to take a trip in the Cessna 195. The 195 was powered by a Jakob's radial engine, which shook the airplane's cowling. Bowman happened to be at Wells that morning and, being the rascal he was, remarked, "There goes vibrating Billy flying the shaky Jake!"

If Salem's were found in a cockpit ashtray, it meant avionics tech George Clobes had been working there.

Cap'n Haines enjoys a Viceroy at the controls of the 500.

Due to the expansion of the Kwik Shops into Nebraska, Iowa, and Illinois and the addition of Calhoun's clothing stores, a Cessna 421 was added to the fleet.

The 421 was Cessna's top-of-the-line propeller airplane in the late '60s and early '70s. The first of 421's the Dillon's operated was of the first model. It came into service in June of 1974. In 1976, it was moved to City Markets in Grand Junction, CO. Replacing it was the later model "421 B" with a longer nose for baggage space.

Cessna 421B "Golden Eagle"
Photo by Acroterion ⬈ #9

Disaster foiled once again! One of the pilots (who will not be shamed by remaining anonymous) had failed to properly latch the right-side nose baggage door. Shortly after takeoff, the door flew open, and one of the suitcases was sucked out! Fortunately, again, it did not strike any part of the airplane. The pilot immediately returned to the airport and landed safely. The suitcase was found scarred but intact, with no damage to the contents. The pilot latched the baggage door securely, completing the flight without any further embarrassing incidents.

A Cessna 402 "Business Liner" was also added to the fleet at about this time. It was also similar in appearance to the 421 but was not pressurized. It was configured as a passenger hauler and used by many Commuter Airlines.

Cessna 402B Business Liner
Photo from San Diego Air & Space Museum ⬈ #10

Both airplanes were used extensively by Dillon Stores, Kwik Shops, and Calhoun's during the 1970s.

Roger Humiston's brother, Dennis, had learned to fly as well. Wanting something different to fly, Dennis bought a PT-17 Stearman.

Dennis Humiston's "Stearman."

Dennis kept the Stearman at Wells. Ace came by one day as it was sitting in front of the Wells lobby. Ace curiously looked it over and asked Haines who it belonged to. Haines told him and asked if he would like to fly it. Ace replied, "No, those things are part of a past life."

In November 1972, Bowman and Sims were dropped off in St. Louis, MO, for ground school in the operating systems on the Sabre 40A. It is a complex airplane with electrically activated, hydraulically operated systems. Electric circuit breakers are all over the cockpit. Hydraulic systems rely on a single pump. Both men were amazed and confused but made it through and looked forward to getting into the airplane.

Bowman also received this certificate.

Having been dropped off by a company plane enroute to somewhere near St. Louis, they were to fly to Wichita on Frontier Airlines with one-way tickets. It is at this time of initial sky-jackings by most perpetrators with one-way tickets. Frontier had no jet-way to board the airplane. Passengers had to exit the terminal through a door to the ramp and climb stairs into the airplane. As they walked across the ramp with other passengers, they were pulled aside by airport police and placed up against the wall of the terminal! They were questioned and frisked, then released to board. On the airplane, they were greeted with skeptical stares as they walking to their seats. Nearing their seats, Bowman bent down to one elderly lady with a most unfriendly glare and said BOO! At first, there was a brief moment of silence, then laughter from those nearby! Fortunately, none of the crew observed this, and the glaring lady also had a good sense of humor.

In January of 1973, Haines got word from Mr. Adams that he had taken into his inventory a Sabre 40 once owned by Travelers Ins, Co. It was an early model, but it would be one he and Sims could be rated in with little differences from the 40A. Haines negotiated a rental contract with Mr. Adams for the use of the Sabre 40. He then contacts Crumm as to whom he and Sims could get training from. Crumm recommended another former Air Force vet who ran his own training company exclusively in Sabreliners.

This person was William "Bill" Burks, Sabreliner Specialist. His business was located in Dallas, TX, but he would travel to his customer's location to perform the training.

Haines received the same Certificate.

Some of Burk's training aids.

Forget to check hydraulic Pressure?

Haines and Sims went into training on Jan. 6 and earned their type ratings on Jan. 19.

The first company trip in the Traveler's Sabre was to Grand Junction with Sims as captain and Bowman as first officer. Haines and Humiston followed in the Howard 500. As the Sabre departed for Hutchinson, the hydraulic pump went offline after gear retraction. The pump wasn't needed to complete the flight, but Bowman seemed nervous about it. After a while, the pump was reset, and the flight continued without further incident.

When payday came around, Bowman became upset when the raise Haines had promised was not there. The fault was not with Haines but the secretary, who had forgotten to update the amount. The secretary, pleading with Bowman, admitted her mistake and apologized profusely. But Bowman had nothing to do with it and placed the blame squarely on Haines. The two had words, and Bowman left in a huff, saying, "I'll never work for you again!"

Haines was upset with Bowman's decision to leave Wells Aircraft. The two had been friends for many years. Sims tried to mediate the dispute with Bowman but without success. Bowman's resolve was firm.

Haines and Sims thought about it for a while and decided that Bowman may have been intimidated by the Sabreliner and used the pay error as an excuse to leave and not be assigned to crew it. Sims was now assigned to be Mr. Carey's pilot.

Although the relationship between Bowman and Sims was tense for a while, they remained on speaking terms. After some time had passed, the two resumed their friendship. Bowman eventually softened to his relationship with Haines and was on speaking terms but never flew for Wells or Dillons again.

In mid-February 1973, North American/Rockwell delivered Sabreliner 40-A, N477X, to Wells Aircraft and Dillon Co's Inc. It drew much attention from the Dillon executives, who came out to examine it. Many were looking forward to their first trip in it.

**Dillon's first Sabreliner N477X.
Pictured here in the factory paint scheme.**

Ray Dillon brought his wife Stella out to take a look at it. She was quite disappointed with it. The cabin was much smaller than the Howards' and did not have a lavatory or vanity. As you entered the airplane, you stepped into the baggage area, and on your right was a jump seat that doubled as a non-flushing potty, lovingly referred to as the "Honey Bucket"! Folding dividers to the cockpit and main cabin provided some modicum of privacy.

Well known for her colorful language, she hurled a barrage of profanity at Ray, Ace, Dick, and Haines that would make a drunken sailor blush! "How do you expect us ladies to have any privacy when we have to use the bathroom"? Her descriptive terms will remain unsaid.

When Swanton was in town, he and Bowman would frequent a beer joint a couple of miles west of the airport, which was Bowman's favorite. The CoCo Room was owned by another WWII vet, Bob Miller. Miller was a survivor of the Bataan Death March. Miller's wife, Beverly, ran the bar. The late '60s and early '70s was the era of GoGo girl dancers, and Beverly cashed in on the fad. She would hire girls to perform on a small stage in one corner of the room without poles or cages. The girls would perform from 4 PM to 8 PM to capitalize on those leaving work from Hutchinson's east side industrial area.

Bowman had the face of a bulldog and the voice of Lewis Armstrong, but the young performers liked him. He was never forward or threatening to them but knew how to make them laugh. Knowing they were often poor, he would leave a generous tip in the dancer's tip jar. He would sometimes entertain the bar's patrons and the dancers as he stood at the bar. Pretending to tuck in his shirt, he would "accidentally" drop his pants, exposing his boxer shorts and sock suspenders!

Tragically, Bob Bowman passed away unexpectedly in his sleep in November 1973. Bowman's legacy is in a book he wrote about his time in the service. The book is titled "Memoirs of a Pilot". It is available at the Hutchinson Public Library.

The movie "Snakes on a Plane" could very well have been taken from an event at Wells Aircraft. Tal Miller bought an Aero Commander to be inspected at Wells for sale by his company. The airplane came from somewhere in the swamps of Louisiana. While removing the floors to examine the flight control mechanisms, the mechanic, Frank Barr, saw a snake slither through a bulkhead from a section uncovered to another that had not yet been uncovered! Barr couldn't get out of there fast enough. He exited the airplane yelling, "Snake, Snake!" How did it get in there? It had to be through the nose gear of the unpressurized Commander.

Taking no chances that someone is bitten, Hephner consulted an exterminator to handle the situation. The airplane sat in the nearly deserted hangar for two days before the exterminators arrived. They set traps and fumigated the plane but never discovered a snake carcass or saw it escape. It is thought that the snake escaped by how it got in between the time of discovery and attempts to exterminate began. Besides, no one even wanted to be in or near the hangar at the time!

Many junior pilots went on to bigger and better things during the seventies.

Jim Little went to Kansas City to fly a King Air.

Gene Kubin went to Plainview, Texas, to fly a Beech Baron.

Humiston went to Koch to fly Lear Jets, then to Dallas, where he started his own business. He later went on to fly the Gulfstream line of jets. He was once featured in an Airplane Repo TV show episode repossessing one of the Gulfstream jets!

Brice Riechert went to TWA.

Randy Stapleton – unknown.

Mike Green is flying King Air ambulances for Mercy Flights of Wichita.

Brian Friesen – ARCO of Dallas, flying the Gulfstream jets.

Merlin "Skip" Mills goes to Borton Inc., a local construction company that has purchased the Dillon Cessna 402.

Gary Crow, a transfer from Skycraft line service, earned his commercial and flight instructor ratings and joined the flight department of Wells Aircraft in November of 1973 as a flight instructor. Then, in 1974, as a charter pilot. Crow had been employed by Skycraft since 1964, working his way through his ratings with aspirations of becoming a pilot. As a flight instructor, Gary was well-liked by his students.

Joe Hill, another young local man, also came on board at this time. He was a likable fellow, full of charisma and confidence. Haines liked him, took him under his wing, and taught him a lot about flying. Haines would let him fly the left seat in the Sabre and the "3s" despite his lack of time and experience!

In 1976, Ace decided Frank Prinster, President of City Markets, should have a pressurized cabin airplane. The Dillon Co's Inc. Cessna 421 was moved to Grand Junction, and the Cessna 402 was sold.

In the summer of 1976, Haines and Aircraft Engine Service landed a contract with the FAA to re-engine their retiring DC-3s. The work has to be done outside on the ramp in front of AES with no shade but what the airplane provided. Haines sent Hephner and a crew of mechanics to perform the work.

The FAA's DC-3's were used for checking Airways and Instrument Landing navigation facilities.

Despite Hephner's crusty character, he realized this was stressful for his men in the heat of July. So, he bought some beer for them to enjoy at break time!

Before   **During**

After the "Break."

General aviation (Gen-Av) was in its heyday in the seventies. General Aviation is "all aviation activities outside of Military or Scheduled Airline Operations." More Gen-Av airplanes were manufactured in this era than any other. Haines and his associates were seemingly buying and selling planes every day!

Going to work at Wells was always exciting because you never knew what might be sitting on the ramp when you walked around the hangar corner.

Late Spring 1977

Sure enough, there it is, "Surprise!" Something new and unusual arrives in Kansas. The author does not know where this PBY came from and who flew it to Wells. However, it is known that Gardener was the purchaser. Gardener sent Swanton to fly it to the Philippines. Swanton was to test-fly it before closing the deal and took Haines with him. Haines later remarked, "Takeoff, climb, cruise, approach, and landing speeds were all the same. The only change to the phases of flight were the "power settings for each"!

The PBY was not the only seaplane to be at Wells. A Grumman Widgeon was given a pre-purchase inspection for a customer of Mr. Adams.

Another of Gardener's pilots was Bob Holt, also a WWII vet. He was a charming fellow who could imitate the accent of many languages. He would often carry on a four-way conversation with himself using the British, German, Japanese, and American southern drawl accents. The four characters throw insults at each other and respond in a huff! He would do this routine with Bowman and Swanton at the CoCo Room, cracking up all those within-ear shot. He could have had his own standup comedy act. Sims was in awe of these characters and often accompanied them to the CoCo Room.

As with Ace, none of these WWII vets spoke of the war. They just enjoyed being with each other, bantering, joking, poking fun at each other and enjoying the entertainment together.

Holt was sent to ferry a Beech Baron from the US to the Philippines one summer. The airplane had ferry tanks installed at Vic Coss's facility in Oakland, CA. When the time came to depart for Hawaii, Coss observed Holt load the airplane with two six-packs of beer, a small pail, and a length of plastic tubing. When asked what these were for, Holt responded, "I plan to drink the beer, and when I have to, I'll pee in the pail. When the pail is half full, I'll put one end of the tubing out the pilot's window opening and the other in the pail. The airflow outside the window will dry the pail, and I can start all over!"

Coss asked, "Won't the urine invade the tail feathers, and its acidity cause corrosion"? Holt replied, "No, in the part of the world I'm flying to, rain showers are quite prevalent, and the urine will be washed away as I fly through them"!

Late in the '70s, Aircraft Engine Service had trouble getting parts from Pratt and Whitney of Canada needed to overhaul their engines. While attending a convention in New York, Ace permitted Haines to fly to Montreal, Canada, to meet with Pratt and Whitney officials. Haines meets with Lucien Lavagar, a vice president in charge of distribution, to discuss the problem.

Lavagar explained to Haines that Pratt and Whitney had decided to concentrate their operations on turbine engines and were phasing out their reciprocating engine support. The company was selling off its radial engine tooling to large rebuilders who had come to them earlier and proposed a buy-out of the tooling. Haines told Lavagar that Aircraft Engine Service could also be interested in bidding on the tooling. Lavagar then gave Haines a list of the tooling still to be sold and the protocols to file bids.

Haines passed this information on to Ace. Seeing the future and Dillon Co.'s. Inc., already in the turbine age with visions of more turbine aircraft in its fleet, Ace and the Dillon Board decided not to invest in acquiring the needed tooling. Aircraft Engine Service was then divested as the operations costs were too high due to parts costs.

Gary Crow and the "London Fog"

It's spring in Kansas, with cool mornings and warm afternoons—coats or jackets are required in the morning, and short sleeves in the afternoon. Crow was the first officer on a flight to Denver with Haines in the Sabre on one such day. On returning to Hutchinson, Crow discovered a London Fog coat that one of the passengers had forgotten. Taking it to Haines, Haines told him to hang it in the lobby, and the owner would claim it. If no one does, you can have it.

Summer came and went, and no one has claimed the coat. Mid-fall and the same cool mornings and warm afternoons. The coat fit Crow, so he claimed it. Again, assigned as FO with Haines, he was tending the steps to the Sabre while wearing the coat as Ace Dillon was boarding, turned, and said, "Nice coat, Gary, I used to have one just like it!"

Haines told Sims later that he had never seen anyone sweat bullets like Crow did that day! Returning to Hutch, Ace got off the plane and never said a word about the coat. Did Ace know, or did he forget it was his? We will never know. Haines said it was like letting the air out of a balloon when the tension of fear left Crow!

In June 1978, Miller purchased a Beech H-18 from Two Bar Ranch out of Wyoming. It had just undergone a pre-purchase inspection by Wells. Its N-number is N22BR. Miller had a customer in Denver who might be interested in buying the airplane.

Asked if Haines could fly it out to Denver, Haines replied, "Yes, I'll have Sims do it." Sims had requested time off to attend the US Open golf tournament at Cherry Hills Country Club in Denver. Sims, his wife Susie, and a longtime friend, Eddie Martinez, an employee of Dillon Stores, were to drive to Denver for the event. Haines explained the situation to Sims and offered the airplane for the trip to Denver. Sims asked, "What if the customer were to buy the plane?" Haines said, "Miller has demo-ed many planes to this person, and they never buy one. They just don't want to pay for a charter flight because the demo is at fuel cost only"!

Twin Beech "N22BR"

The flight to Denver was made on a Thursday. Sims stayed at an airport hotel used by the Dillon pilots on company trips. Martinez stayed with his aunt and uncle in Arvada, a suburb of Denver. The aunt and uncle operated a Buick, Pontiac, and GMC dealership there.

Sims had rented a compact car for transportation around town. When it arrived at the general aviation terminal, it became apparent that it was too small. Arrangements were made to rent a larger car, and they all, with baggage, piled into the small car for the drive to the rental agency. While enroute, the driver was very nonchalant, with one hand on the steering wheel, the other out the driver's window, and asking what we were in town for. Sims, in the front seat, told him and asked him if he had heard of golfer Lee Travino. He replied, "Yeah, he's one of the big names". Sims said, "Well, that's Eddie Travino in the back seat, Lee's brother." The young driver immediately sat up in his seat, put both hands on the wheel, and was very courteous for the rest of the trip!

Martinez's aunt and uncle, Rosie and Ron Goodman, were congenial. They often joked with and poked fun at each other and those around them.

Other friends of Sims were there for the tournament, too. On Friday, the men played a round of golf at a public course while the ladies went shopping.

All attended the tournament on Saturday and Sunday. On Saturday, they followed Travino and others around the course. On Sunday, after walking the course on Saturday, they decided to go directly to the observation bleachers adjacent to hole #16 to observe all competitors. Directly behind the bleachers were restrooms and a concession stand.

Martinez's aunt was a very attractive lady. On Sunday, she was dressed in all black: low heels, shorts, a halter top, and a floppy-brimmed hat. The group was seated on the top row of the bleachers. Midway through the day, Ron turned to Rosie and said, "Honey, I'm hungry; why don't you go down, turn a couple of tricks, and get us a hot dog and some beer?" Everyone within earshot was aghast! But that was just Rosie and Ron pranking the crowd and enjoying the reaction it provoked!

After a weekend of fun, there was a message for Sims to call Haines. Haines told Sims, "Sorry Mike, they bought the airplane and flew it up to Boulder, where it will be based."

Now what? After changing Martinez's work schedule, they were counting on the airplane to have them back in Hutchinson by noon on Monday. They couldn't rest, rent another car, or drive to Hutchinson on time. Martinez was scheduled to be back at work early Monday afternoon. Fortunately, they booked an early flight to Wichita on Continental Airlines. Haines arranged to have them picked up and flown to Hutchinson in one of Wells Aircraft's planes. Martinez made it to work on time, and life is good!

1978: Time Savers Convenience stores of Louisiana join Dillon Co's. Inc. Based in New Orleans, Dillon flights are now flown into Lake Front airport, which extends into Lake Pontchartrain.

1979: Ray E. Dillon Sr. retires. Ray E. Dillon Jr. becomes Chairman of the Board, Dick Dillon becomes President of Dillon Co's Inc., and Paul Dillon is Senior Vice President.

In the Fall of 1979, Sims and Crow were assigned to fly Ross Beech (no relation to the Beech Aircraft Co.) to Nashville, TN. Mr. Beech is a Dillon Co. board member who owns a communications company affiliated with the CBS network. The purpose of the trip is to attend the Country Music Awards program for 1979, which CBS is broadcasting. Mr. Beech has generously provided Sims and Crow tickets to the show at the (new) Grand Old Opry.

Sims and Crow were seated close to the stage. Crow is to the left of Sims, and to the left of Crow are several empty seats. As the program started, some ladies were seated next to Crow. The lady next to Crow turns out to be June Carter, Johnny Cash's wife!

There are television monitors located on each side of the stage. At one point in the program, the Carter Sisters are recognized, and the cameras panned the ladies moving toward June. Sims and Crow are nudging each other in glee, thinking they will be on national TV! But no, the panning stops as June is recognized and acknowledged. The pilots glee turns to disappointment, but both enjoy the experience!

Beechcraft Model 90 King Air.
Photo by Acroterion ⌗ #11
Photo represents Beechcraft Models A, B, C & E – 90's

April 2, an A-90 King Air is added to the fleet in Hutchinson. June 19, an E-90 King Air replaces the A90 in Hutchinson, and the A90, at the incessant pleading of pilot Lincoln Hall, replaces the Cessna 421 in Grand Junction, CO.

As the '70s wind down, the flight school is slowing down. The GI Bill for flight training of Viet Nam era veterans has expired, and it was a good part of the school's business. Most of the young instructors have moved on from Wells Aircraft, having built flight time and experience for their resumes.

Due to the growth of Gen-Av during the '70s, more regulations were enacted and imposed on GA operations. Not all are bad. Those that addressed safety issues were mostly welcomed. Some, however, were deemed punitive. Financial restrictions were made regarding non-business use of company aircraft and non-company personnel who ride on company-owned planes being used for business purposes.

Along with new regulations, insurance rates rose due to increased industry litigation levels. Aircraft operators were faced with substantial liability obligations if involved in an accident resulting in loss of life and extensive property damage. Obscene punitive damages were levied if an entity was found guilty of gross negligence.

During the late '70s and the '80s, corporate raiders bought up undervalued companies and sold off their assets for profit.

Dillon Company pilots began transporting University of Kansas officials from Lawrence to Hutchinson. These guests included the Dean of Kansas University's Business College, Joseph Pichler, and other business professors for meetings with Dillon Co's Inc. Officers and Board members. At this time, Dillon Co's Inc. stock was undervalued and could be a target for a leveraged buyout. Ace, Dick and Paul Dillon, Joseph Pichler, other KU Professors, and the Dillon board devised a plan to prevent a hostile takeover.

Of course, the Dillon pilots are curious but oblivious to what is happening. However, what was about to happen will become evident in the future!

Chapter Five: The 80's More Growth with Kroger

On January 1, Gary Crow resigned from Wells Aircraft and joined commuter airline "Air Midwest."

With the exodus of the younger pilots, Wells Aircraft and Dillon Co. once again used contract pilots and put Mr. Hephner into service as a pilot.

One contactor was Richard Kukuk. He lived in Oklahoma City and was based at Wiley Post Airport. Rockwell/Commander Corp. employed Kukuk until it was sold to Israeli Aircraft Industries. In the past, he came to Wells and trained pilots to fly the Turbo Commander while on Dillon Co. trips. Kukuk owned a beautiful Beech Debonair, which he kept in immaculate condition. He would use the Debonair to commute between Wiley Post and Hutchinson. Wells Aircraft would pay for the fuel used and time put on the Debonair.

Another contract pilot was Bob Park of Skiatook, Oklahoma. Oral Roberts Ministries employed park at one time and flew a Falcon 20. Park was 100% Cherokee Native American. Park would sometimes commute by auto and others by Haines, sending an airplane to pick him up.

Park had colorful tales to tell while employed by Roberts. Roberts shared his airplane with Jimmy Swaggart, another televangelist related to rocker Jerry Lee Lewis. Park relates to Haines that once on loan to Swaggart, Lewis was the passenger to be flown. Lewis was under the influence of alcohol or another substance and showed up for the trip with his newlywed wife (his 14-year-old cousin) wielding a gun! Park, scared that Lewis might shoot him, insisted that Lewis put the gun in his luggage and store it in the baggage compartment. At first, Lewis declined to comply, waving the gun around. But Park explained that if that gun were to be fired while in flight, it could cause damage to the airplane, and all could die as a result! Lewis finally relented, and the gun was placed in the baggage compartment.

Another time, Park and Haines are on a trip together and watching the news on TV when Swaggart condemns fellow evangelist Jim Baker for infidelity! Park tells Haines, "What a hypocrite, Swaggart has seen the inside of more whore houses than he has churches!"

In mid-1980, Haines tried to find a full-time pilot to be based in Hutchinson. Having no luck finding a local candidate, Haines placed an ad in Trade-A-plane, a nationwide publication, with a job description and requirements for the position.

In October of 1980, Haines phone interviewed Donald Beaton—a retired Naval aviator from Alabama. Beaton was a Navy P-3 "Orion" flight engineer, a submarine patrol version of the Lockheed "Electra" airliner. During his time in service, Beaton earned his civilian pilot ratings, which met Haines's requirements, and Beaton agreed to move to Hutchinson if hired.

Haines flew Beaton via airlines to Wichita, had Sims pick him up, and flew to Hutchinson. After an in-person interview, Haines had Sims take him for an evaluation flight in the E-90 King Air. Beaton does a fine job, and Sims tells Haines he would be a good fit for Wells Aircraft and Dillons. Beaton was hired and began work in November of 1980.

Joseph A. Pichler was named Executive Vice President of Dillon Co. Inc. Pichler is the first company officer not from the Dillon family. This possibly explained the trips to Lawrence, but there was more to come!

Haines and Sims had now been working together for over a decade. Their professional relationship was well established, but the men also became friends. Haines enjoyed making fun of and embarrassing Sims in harmless ways. Sims would often find ways to get even with Haines.

On one trip, they were having lunch at a hotel buffet. Sims was the only person at the buffet line when a hapless young lady bussing tables walked by and lost control of her tray. The tray and its contents crashed to the floor. Haines, seizing the moment, boomed at Sims, "Must you always cause a scene?"

It wasn't much later when Sims got his revenge. The two were on a trip to Oakland, CA, in the summer of 1981 and stayed at the Oakland Hilton Airport hotel. This was a full-service hotel with a large bar room and separate dining area. Near the hotel was the headquarters of the Oakland Raiders football team.

Late in the afternoon, Haines called Sims, and the two went for a beer in the bar before going to dinner. They sat at a table at the rear of the room even though few people were in the bar. The bar was "L" shaped with the long side-oriented North/South and the short side to the West.

Not long after they were there, John Matuszak and Ted Hendricks walked in. The two Raiders sat at the short side of the bar near the jukebox. Both men order shots of a clear drink, Vodka or Gin. As they were being served, Matuszak went to the jukebox, put money in, and selected some music. Evidently, it wasn't loud enough for him, so it appeared he picked up the jukebox, reached behind it, and turned up the volume!

Haines, jokingly, tells Sims to go over to the two huge defensive football players and ask them to turn the volume down! Without expression or hesitation, Sims gets up and goes over to them. They had won the Super Bowl over the Eagles 27 to 10 earlier in the year. Sims congratulates them on a great game and points to Haines, saying they want to buy them their next shots. They look at Haines, thank Sims, and return to their drinks.

At the table, Haines asks Sims, "What did you tell them?" Sims replies, "I told them if they didn't turn the volume down, you were going to kick their asses!"

Back in Oakland sometime later, Haines had again embarrassed Sims somehow. While looking for a Quik Stop store, they were unknowingly driving through the city's red-light district. Haines was driving, and Sims was riding shotgun when they hit a red light. On the corner next to their car stood an obvious hooker. Coincidently, the tune "Come and Get Your Love" by Redbone was playing on the radio.

Not letting this opportunity go by, Sims noticed the light for cross traffic had turned yellow, ducked down while rolling the window down, and turned up the volume just as the "Come and get your Love" lyric played! Haines smacked Sims on the shoulder and said, "Damn you!" Fortunately, the light turned green before the hooker could get to the car. Later, both had a good laugh!

In July 1981, Crow left Air Midwest and went to Koch Industries.

Swanton is back in town. Haines needed someone to chase him to Two Jacks in Olive Branch, MS. Haines needed to see Mr. Adams and take a pre-purchase airplane to him. Haines and Swanton arrive in time for lunch. Mr. Adams had joined the Sheriff Department and had a Ford Bronco equipped with a red light and siren. Swanton noticed this enroute to lunch, and the child in him surfaced. He asked Mr. Adams to turn them on. He did so, and Swanton was ecstatic, hooting and hollering during the short time they were on. Swanton thanked Mr. Adams and said, "I've always wanted to do that!"

1982: Ace, for some reason, was flying on the airlines and not on the company planes. Something was going on, and whether Haines knew what it is or not is unknown. If he did, he kept it a particularly good secret.

Early in 1982, Hall badgered Haines to replace the A90 with an E90 King Air. Haines does so. Dillon is now an all-turbine fleet. save for the 421B, two King Airs and the Sabreliner.

Then, a seemingly emergency flight in mid-November is made to Cincinnati, OH. Prior to the flight, Sims asks Haines, "What is in Cincinnati?" Haines just shook his head as if he didn't know. Sims was preparing for the flight when he remembered the flight from Teterboro, NJ, when the Howard 500 outran the Gulfstream 1 of Kroger, which was headed to Cincinnati a decade ago! Sims then asks Haines, "Kroger?" Haines smiles and goes about his business.

Ace and the Dillon Executives had devised a plan to merge with the larger Kroger chain. After negotiations, both parties agreed that Dillon Co's. Inc. would become a wholly owned subsidiary of Kroger. The merger was announced and voted on by the stockholders approving the merger.

Upon the announcement, Ace assured the Dillon flight department that this merger would mean more flights and to a nationwide area.

Joe Pichler becomes President of Dillon Co's. Inc.

The merger was made in early 1983 and would allow Dillon Co's. Inc. to keep its own management structure but be under the guidance of the Kroger Board. Ace and Dick Dillon, along with Pichler, join the Kroger Board of Directors.

This is a brilliant move for Dillons. It prevents a possible hostile takeover of the company and saves thousands of jobs. However, many skeptics in Hutchinson believed Dillon was trying to buy out Kroger! Grocery prices would skyrocket! None of which is true or happened.

On this first flight to Cincinnati, Haines and Sims meet the Kroger Chief Pilot and Flight Department manager, Carl Simons, and the Kroger pilots. All are welcoming and friendly. The Kroger fleet of airplanes consists of a Dassault Falcon 10, a Cessna Citation II, and a Mitsubishi MU 300 "Diamond" jet.

The Kroger Flight Department proudly calls the Cincinnati Municipal Airport "Lunken Field" its home. Nestled amidst rolling bluffs, Lunken boasts a unique location with the Ohio River and its Kentucky bluffs bordering its southern edge. Pilots approaching from the north enjoy the most favorable conditions, while departures are best made in the same direction. With the dawn of the jet age, a new airport, "Greater Cincinnati Airport," emerged in nearby Covington, Kentucky. This shift led to Lunken's transformation into a bustling hub for general aviation, welcoming numerous corporate fleets. Today, Lunken's rich history lives on through its preserved airline terminal, earning it the affectionate nickname "Sunken Lunken."

Kroger's fleet is housed in an unusual hangar called the "Caterpillar Hangar." It appeared to be a dinosaur-sized caterpillar if there was such a thing. But Kroger was not there long as they were building their hangar—a large two-hanger building with offices connecting the two. It resembles Wells Aircraft but on a larger scale.

The south side of the complex would house the Kroger Flt. Dept. and the north side leased to other entities. It also has its own fueling facilities.

Wells Aircraft performs the first non-factory de-mate of the wing from the fuselage on a Lear Jet. It was time for this critical corrosion inspection, and the owner didn't want to wait on the factory's schedule. Haines and Hephner went to Lear and the FAA and got approval for the procedure.

1983: Ace and Dick Dillon personally buy a King Air 200 and enter a lease agreement with the company for its use.

The King Air 200 N551JL

**Monterey, California Sept. 1983
From left: Caroline Haines, "Bill" Haines, and Mike Sims
One of the last flights in the 40-A Sabreliner.**

1984: The Sabre 40 is traded for Model 60. The 60 is extended, seats two more people, and has a flushing toilet in the rear with a privacy door. Stella Dillon would have been more receptive to this airplane!

The Sabre 60 in Oakland, CA.

1984: Haines is on the phone when he gets a knock on his office door. The secretary/receptionist says, "Sorry to interrupt, but there is a man on line 2 who claims he is John Wayne!" Haines gestures to her that it is okay, and she leaves. Haines terminates his current call and picks up line 2. "This is Haines," he answers. The party on the other end replies, "Mr. Haines, this is John Wayne, and I just put Harry Swanton on a plane to Wichita."

Wayne: "He showed up yesterday at my place with bag and baggage in tow, saying he has retired and going to Hutchinson to live!"

Haines is surprised by this development as this is the first he'd heard of it! Haines visits with Mr. Wayne about the situation, and Wayne also relates that it was the first for him too.

Mr. Wayne ends the conversation with, "Well, good luck. When I put Harry on the plane, he was drunk and carrying his savings on the plane in a grocery bag. I believe it is well north of a hundred grand! He is arriving on flight so and so and at such and such a time and wants someone from Wells Aircraft to pick him up. Just hope and pray he gets off the flight with that grocery bag!"

Swanton gets off the plane with his grocery bag intact. Haines is gracious enough to put him up at his place until he can find a place of his own. Swanton buys a used pickup and rents a small house a mile east of the airport. He gets a dog from the humane society named

'Skeeter.' Skeeter is up in age and adores Swanton. They go together almost everywhere.

Not happy with the rental house, Swanton buys a mid-size travel trailer to live in. At first, he parks it at the Haines property, a farmstead several miles south of town. Not happy with the distance from town, he parks it behind the Dillons' (#3) hangar. This didn't last long, and he wound up at a commercial trailer park with utility hookups.

Sadly, Swanton passed away in 1986. Poor old Skeeter goes back to the humane society, his fate unknown.

In 1984, Tom Thumb convenience stores and Junior Foods of Florida and Alabama joined Dillon Co.'s Inc. They are headquartered in Crestview, FL, on the western end of the Florida panhandle. More demand for the flight dept. as Ace envisioned.

In April 1984, Haines recognized the service of Alvin Sweet with a retirement party in hangar 2. Sweet began his tenure as a line service technician with the City of Hutchinson. At the time, the city controlled fuel sales and used the profits to improve the airport. When Skycraft took over fuel sales, they employed Sweet. Then, when Wells bought out Skycraft, Sweet was retained. First as line service manager and soon after as parts dept. Manager, a position he held until his retirement. Haines hires a belly dancer to entertain Sweet!

Sweet poses with the "Belly Dancer" at his retirement Party!

Haines hires another contract pilot, Hans Mulders. Mulders is a former Royal Dutch Airforce pilot who flew the Douglas "Skyraider" attack aircraft. At the time when he joined Wells, he was a Range Flyer Ferry pilot out of Wichita, KS., delivering airplanes all over the world. Mulders would become the owner of Range Flyers shortly after joining Wells.

Hans Mulders prepares to install ferry tanks.

By this time, aircraft sales had slowed drastically, and Haines began accompanying Mulders on some international flights. On one occasion, Haines and his wife, Caroline, flew in semi-formation with Mulders, delivering two King Air 300s to China!

August 1984: Gary Crow leaves Koch, Ind., and is hired by Collins, and. as a contractor for Wells Aircraft. In April 1985, Collins, a Limousines, Ambulances, and School Bus manufacturer, purchased a Sabreliner Model 40. Crow is now full-time with Collins, and Sims Type rates him in the Sabre in May. Crow hires Max Murry as the first officer. Murry is a Hutchinson native and ex-military pilot.

Collins Sabre 40, N325K

In early 1985, Jan Mann had a customer for a Sabreliner 40. The customer is a Chilean arms manufacturer who is selling its products to Iraqi dictator Saddam Hussein. Haines locates a Sabre 40, and he and Mann pitch it to the customer. It is sold with the agreement to train three pilots to fly it. One of those pilots is Carlos Cardoen, the company's founder and owner!

Industrias
División Defensa

"INDUSTRIAS CARDOEN S.A." GUARANTEES THAT THEIR PRICES ARE THE MOST COMPETITIVE IN THE MARKET AND GUARANTEES RAPID DELIVERY AS WELL. CARDOEN ALSO GUARANTEES POST-SALE AND TECHNICAL ASSISTANCE.

Swedish Saab fighter armed with "Cluster Bombs."

CARDOEN Industries initiated the manufacture of military products in 1978 as a contribution of private enterprise to the DEFENSE OF CHILE.

The variety, high quality, and low prices of these products have created a growing international demand and several export transactions have been successfully completed with friendly countries.

At present CARDOEN Industries is working on a number of research and development projects, all of which are oriented to satisfy both domestic and foreign requirements.

Cardoen produces a full line of products ranging from mini grenades, grenades, land mines, conventional bombs, cluster bombs, (now prohibited) missiles and launchers, armored vehicles, and half-track tanks.

At the time, the United States was an ally of Iraq as Iraq was at war with Iran. Although the US was not at war with Iran, Iran had committed acts of terrorism against the US and kidnapping of US citizens, thus the support for Iraq.

Cardoen sends his chief pilot, Gustavo Lapostol, in February, and then in March, pilot Pedro Cifuentes to Hutchinson for introduction to and training in the Sabreliner. At the time of the deal, Sims had no idea he was part of it. He was contracted to train and type rate these two individuals as well as Cardoen, also a pilot, in the Sabreliner!

Chief Pilot Gustavo and Pilot Pedro

Flight training begins in early March for Gustavo Lapostol and mid-March for Pedro Cifuentes (English translation: Pete Fountain). Gustavo speaks broken English, and Pedro very little English. Sims sometimes has to use a form of sign language with Gustavo during training. Then, use Gustavo as an interpreter when training Pedro. Cardoen is fluent in English but cannot attend training sessions at this time and gets his training later. Pedro is the best pilot and takes to the Sabre easily. Despite the language barrier, Gustavo is a good pilot but not as easy to train as Pedro. Carlos is the least experienced of the three, but with his ability to speak English, he adapted readily with few problems.

Gustavo and Pedro's training came along nicely as the two men neared qualification for type ratings. The FAA was contacted about getting the two rated in the United States. They reply that it is impossible to issue a US-type rating if they do not hold a valid US pilot certificate. To obtain a US pilot certificate, one must speak, write, and understand the English language.

It was rumored that Cardoen had contacts at the US State Department and made a plea to them for a waiver of exemption from the FAA rule. Nothing came of the plea; the FAA was not swayed. So, Cardoen contacts the República De Chile Aeronautica Civil, the Chilean equivalent of the FAA. They approved the plan to have Sims, a US pilot, complete the training in Chile. The decision was then made to continue the training in Chile.

Sims gets a passport and packs for a stay in Santiago, Chile. Gustavo, Pedro, and Sims depart Hutchinson for Miami, Florida, on April 6.

April 6, 1985

The three men spend the night with Cardoen, who has a residence in Miami, and the four depart the next day for Chile. The route would take them from Miami through the Maya corridor over Cuba to refuel in Panama City. From there to Quito, Ecuador, to top off with fuel for the flight to Arica, Chile, to clear customs. Then, a short flight to Iquique, Chile, to spend the night.

Sims asks Lapostol, "Why the top off in Quito, and why overnight in Iquique?" Lapostol replies, "Peru and Chile are feuding, and we must fly over international waters to not intrude on their airspace. Even at that, Peru may send up a flight of fighters to look us over. Not to worry, if they do, just smile and wave at them, they don't dare fire on a US airplane! As for the overnight, Cardoen has a bomb factory on the mountain there and wants to go up for a visit."

Sims thought, "Fighter jets, bombs, Haines, what in the hell have you gotten me into!"

The flight legs all went smoothly. The Peruvians did not send up any fighters. The winds at Arica and Iquique were from the north, and both landings were made to the north after dark. Lapostol turned from left base to final a little to the left of the centerline, then lined up about a quarter mile from the threshold at both airports. Sims asked him, "Why the dogleg in the turn to final?" Lapostol responds, "You'll see why tomorrow morning."

The following day, as the group entered the car to take them to the bomb factory, Sims was amazed at how the Andes Mountains appeared to rise from the Pacific Ocean almost vertically, with just a narrow strip of land at their base. If you overshoot the turn to final, you may have just kissed your ass goodbye!

The bomb factory was at the top of the mountain range above Iquique. The road up the mountain was a narrow zig-zag affair cut out of the side of the mountain. If you met oncoming traffic, you would get as far right as possible if on the mountain side of the road and stop to let those oncoming on the ocean side of the road pass by.

After a factory tour, the group flew to Santiago's Los Cerrillos Airport. The airport is located southwest of metropolitan Santiago and is home to Cardoen's Aviation Department.

Industrias Cardoen Hangar Complex

This facility was once a Cessna dealership but now occupied by Cardoen. It was comprised of a fairly large hangar, a lobby area with a receptionist/secretary, and offices.

Sims was staying at the Santiago Sheraton San Cristobal Hotel just north of downtown. It is a lush, full-service facility with a beautiful view of the city from his room.

**Chilean Convenience Store.
"Kwik Shop?"**

Sims was very grateful for the opportunity to visit these Central and South American nations. Having only visited border cities in Mexico and Canada, I found this trip very educational. Sims discovered Panama City, Quito, and Santiago, which were vibrant cities. In Chile, the vistas were incredible.

However, Sims was sometimes terrified as armed guards protected almost all of Cardoen's facilities. On some occasions, Sims himself was assigned an armed bodyguard! The bodyguard, Sergio, would tell Sims, "Don't go there" or "Go this way," among other instructions. Sims asked Lapostol, "Why all the security?" The reply was, "We are supplying Iraq with weapons to use against Iran, and the Ayatollahs of Iran know where we are. We watch for saboteurs and assassins who may harm us! Not to worry, nothing has happened so far."

Sims thought, "Well, that's some comfort!"

After Sims has completed the training of the three men and it is time for their type rating check rides, they go to the Chilean FAA. To recommend the applicants for the ratings, Sims must obtain a Chilean Pilots Certificate and write a letter of recommendation for each of the three. The Chilean officials are very accommodating and issue Sims the required credentials.

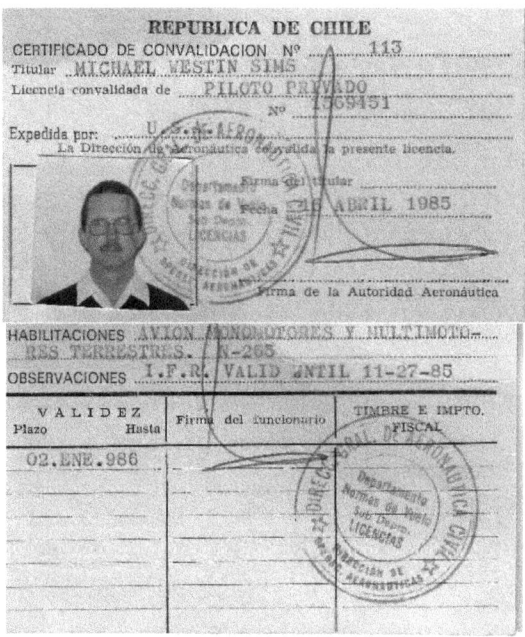

Sims's Chilean Pilots Certificate.

All three men pass their oral exams and flight proficiency tests on their first attempts.

In celebration, Cardoen treats everyone to dinner at the Santiago Country Club.

Cardoen later, at great expense, built a munitions factory in Iraq. Unfortunately, Saddam betrayed him by nationalizing the factory and sending Cardoen and his management team out of Iraq!

In 1985, Joe Pichler was named executive vice president of Kroger, and David Dillon, Paul Dillon's son, was named President and CEO of Dillon Co's Inc.

Dillon adds a Cessna Citation 501-SP (Single Pilot) to its fleet. All pilots, including maintenance manager Hephner, are type-rated to fly it single pilots.

Turkey Hill Dairy and Turkey Hill Minit Markets of Lancaster, Pennsylvania, join Dillon Co's Inc.

Due to expansion, Simons hired an ex-TWA pilot to join the Kroger flight department. It is unknown why this pilot left TWA. He is believed to be in his forties when he joined Kroger, well below retirement age. He was thought to be the First Officer of a TWA 727 that was highjacked and flown to Beirut, Lebanon.

Having not been with Kroger for very long, he went to the Kroger Board and accused Simons of running an unsafe flight department! He is very convincing, and Simons and the Kroger vice president overseeing the flight dept. are fired!

A few days later, Mr. TWA (from now on referred to as Mr. T) was named Kroger's Chief Pilot and Flight Dept. manager. Haines recognizes that this man is on a mission to make a name for himself in the Who's Who in Corporate Aviation! Haines warns, "Watch your Ps and Qs around this guy; you could be next to get the ax!"

Since joining Kroger, the Dillon Flight Department has been buying fuel from the local FBO, Signature Services, at Lunken; then, after Mr. T is in charge of things in Cincinnati, he comes to Haines and says, "I have been instructed to instruct you to obtain your fuel from our facilities!"

Dillon begins fueling at the Kroger facility after that. The King Air and Citation are no problem, but the single-point refueling pressure is marginal for the Sabreliner. At times, it causes an imbalance of fuel in the wings, requiring over-the-wing refueling to correct it. When this occurs, the fuel caps at the wing tips must be opened. Because there is air pressure in the unfull tank, opening it must be done with caution. There is a flapper valve that must be depressed after removal of the cap itself. The pressure inside will cause a geyser of fuel mist and droplets, hazardous to man and machine!

A few months later, Mr. T came to Haines and said, "I was in error about the fuel situation. You must purchase your fuel from Signature Services!" It seems he didn't consult the contract with the City Airport

Authority, which states, "Kroger may fuel only those aircraft owned and registered to the Kroger Company." The Dillon airplanes are technically owned and registered to Dillon Co's Inc., a wholly owned subsidiary!

From then on, Dillon flights to Cincinnati parked their airplanes at Signature Services and fueled with them.

1985: Don Beaton, a Navy retiree, joins the Naval Yacht Club on Treasure Island Naval Station just north of the San Francisco/Oakland Bay bridge.

**Treasure Island US Naval Station.
Photo courtesy of the U.S. Navy**

On Bay Area trips, Beaton would take sailing lessons at the yacht club. After his certification as a "Sailboat Operator" by the club, Beaton would rent a sailboat by the hour and sail around San Francisco Bay. Sometimes, he would take the other pilots who were willing to sail with him.

Don Beaton sailing San Fransico Bay with Angel Island in the background.

1986. Loaf 'N Jug convenience stores of Colorado join Dillon Co's Inc., headquartered in Pueblo, CO.

1986. Haines prepares an ad to be placed in various aviation publications.

The ad application contained the following dialog:

Wells Aircraft is affiliated with Range Flyers of Wichita, KS. Our maintenance and avionics shops have prepared many different aircraft for ferry crossing over the Atlantic and Pacific routes. These aircraft include but are not limited to Beech models 55, 60, 90, and 200. Range Flyers and Wells Aircraft Inc. have done most of the 1900 airplanes for export by Beech Aircraft Corp.

Hans Mulders is president of Range Flyers and has many years of experience and expertise in the ferry business. Hans is well known to almost all Beech Distributors around the world.

AIRCRAFT SALES

Wells Aircraft has specialized in buying and selling preowned aircraft for many years. Our sales aircraft are certified up to date and airworthy by our maintenance dept, guaranteeing satisfaction. Our customers are individuals and corporations. This is why they rely on Wells Aircraft to do what we do best!

Haines and Mulders were to select a few photos to insert in the ad, but somehow the project was canceled due to liability concerns.

Before the Kroger merger, Haines ran an ad in the *"Cross Country News,"* a monthly publication by two veteran Women's Army Air Corps ladies based out of Addison Airport, Addison, TX.

1987. Haines tells Sims to Type rate Hephner in the Sabreliner. Sims tells Hephner, "You must remember, you can't jump out of the pilot's seat and go outside to fix a problem. Remember the image of your idea of a perfect aircraft mechanic! You can only fix inflight problems from the cockpit." Hephner passes the Type check without undoing his seat belt!

1987. Mini Mart, Inc. of Casper, WY. Join Dillon Co's Inc. They operate stores in Wyo., Col., Neb., SD., ND and Mont. More area to cover for the flight dept.!

1987. Collins Industries sells its Sabreliner and puts a Beechcraft B-100 King Air into service.

Gary Crow with Collins B-100 King Air.

Charles (Chuck) and Alice Fry of Fry's Markets live in Arizona during the winter and Northern California during the summer. They like the Dillon Co's Sabre 60 and buy one for personal use. Only needing the airplane occasionally, they base it at Wells Aircraft and hire Dillon and Wells pilots to crew it.

The Fry's Sabreliner 60 N607CF

In the late summer of 1987, Haines was having pain in his left side and down his left leg. He thought it might be sciatica and went to Doctor Jack Perkins, also the Airman's Medical Examiner, for diagnosis. Perkins believes there might be something else going on and orders some tests. Unfortunately, Haines is diagnosed with pancreatic cancer.

Ace arranges for Dillon Co's Inc. to fly Haines and his wife to Houston, TX, to see a medical firm specializing in pancreatic cancer. Sadly, they confirm Perkins diagnosis and identify it as an aggressive and fatal form, which means Haines has only a few months to live.

Oct. 1986: Last known photo of William F. Haines. Haines is holding his Granddaughter.

Ace is informed of the situation. Even though he gave up his position as Dillon Co.'s Inc. President and CEO, he remained President of Wells Aircraft Inc. Learning of Haines's condition, Ace, out of appreciation of Haines's service, appointed Haines President of Wells Aircraft Inc.

Hephner knew of Haines's plight; he flew him to Houston in the Citation. The Dillon and Wells pilots and the rest of Wells employees were totally unaware of what was happening with Haines.

Haines didn't come to his office for a couple of days after the flight to Houston. Before coming to the office, Haines calls Sims out to the farm for a talk. After explaining to Sims his situation, Sims replies, "Damn it, Haines, don't you dare die on me; I can't lose you as a friend. Besides, the place will be chaotic without your wisdom and leadership!"

Haines puts up a gallant fight against the cancer but succumbs to it on November 3, 1987. He is only 57 years old.

Although he was not at Wells for several days before his passing, things were solemn around the airport and Wells after his passing!

He served the Dillon Co. admirably for 30 years. He elevated the Company to a worldwide market through his entrepreneurship with Wells Aircraft. In recognition of his accomplishments, Richard Dillon and Merl "Mert" Sellers commissioned a bronze plaque in his image, recognizing his contribution to aviation commerce in Hutchinson as a "PROMINENT AVIATOR." It is displayed in the foyer of the Hutchinson Municipal Airport Terminal building.

**Photo courtesy of The Hutchinson News
Wednesday, April 13, 1988**

Late Hutch aviator honored

By Jerry Maxfield
The Hutchinson News

A few minutes after 10 a.m. Wednesday, Carolyn Haines gently tugged the cover from a bronze plaque in the foyer of Hutchinson Municipal Airport.

Mrs. Haines, of rural Haven, acknowledged the applause of about 60 people gathered for the unveiling of the plaque, which honors her late husband, prominent Hutchinson aviator William F. Haines.

Haines, 56, died Nov. 3, 1987, at his home.

His aviation career spanned 40 years, and took him from small fabric-covered planes with wooden propellers to the age of business jets.

He had been chief pilot for the Dillon Cos. for 30 years.

"Bill would have been proud of this day," Mrs. Haines told the crowd.

Dozens of area business and civic leaders were on hand for the unveiling of the plaque, which was a project undertaken by Richard Dillon, 4600 East 28th, and Merl Sellers, 119 Kisiwa Parkway.

Dillon, an executive of Dillon Cos., and Sellers, president of Luminous Neon, were both long-time friends of Haines, and Sellers had the plaque produced through his firm.

In remarks just before the unveiling, Dillon told the crowd that Haines was the unofficial leader among local aviators.

"Three men were influential in the development of this airport. Hap Stevens in the beginning, Roland Wells from World War II to the mid '70s, and Bill Haines, who was sort of chairman of the board, so to speak. Bill was a friend to all of us," Dillon said.

Mike Sims, 2502 North Hendricks, has been chief pilot for Dillon Cos. since Haines' death.

"I flew with Bill for 19 years. When I first flew with him we flew an old Lockheed Lodestar, an airplane that today is considered an antique. He was an excellent pilot, and he knew how to teach. He knew how to bring people along. He was a super guy."

Dillon agreed.

"Bill Haines was the kind of guy everybody liked instinctively. He was a friend as well as being the instructor who taught me instrument flying. He was a great guy."

A William F. Haines memorial scholarship fund has been established in Haines' memory at Hutchinson Community College for students pursuing a career in aeronautical engineering.

Courtesy of The Hutchinson News.

With Haines passing, Ace reinstated himself as President of Wells Aircraft Inc. However, Ace needs a Vice President and general manager for Wells Aircraft. He leaves the selection to David Dillon, President and CEO of Dillon Co's Inc.

David Dillon invites Sims to lunch to discuss Wells' leadership. He asks Sims if he would be interested in becoming VP and GM of Wells. Sims replies, "David, I would be a greater asset to the company as Chief Pilot. Jim Hephner has been with Wells and Haines longer than I, and as shop manager, Hephner knows the customer base better than I do."

Sims loved flying and being tied mainly to a desk terrified him!

Dillon makes the same offer to Hephner, who eagerly accepts the position. Hephner then appoints himself as the Fry's Sabreliner pilot with Ms. Anderson as First Officer.

Dean Wedman is promoted to Service Manager in Hephner's place.

1988. Kroger became the target of a hostile takeover. The attempt was made by Dart-Kraft Co. and not by raiders Kravis, Kohlberg, and Roberts. The movie "Barbarians at the Gate" was based on the firm of KKR.

The Kroger board, led by Joe Pichler and Ace, devised a plan to leverage the Kroger Co. themselves. It had never been done before in the supermarket business. Had Safeway, once the nation's largest supermarket chain, done it, it may have survived to be a significant competitor today.

Pilots in both the Kroger and Dillon flight dept's were put on high alert. Pilots were issued pagers to be always available. Many flights were made to accommodate financier's audits and inspections of facilities. Some financiers were very demanding about what amenities be provided on their trips!

The principals only knew the plan's full details, but it entailed buying stockholder shares at a generous amount over the market price. Also offered were options and junk bonds. It was intended to make Kroger too costly for a takeover, a poison pill! This was all done with mostly borrowed money! Hence, the flights of financiers!

It successfully kept Kroger Co. and Dillon Co's Inc. intact and discouraged others from making a run on it!

To reduce debt, the company implemented cost-cutting measures. Fortunately, the flight departments were essential for company executives to oversee operational changes effectively.

1989. All Dillon pilots' type-rated in the Sabre, and Citation must now receive recurrent training with Flight Safety International. Later that year, the requirement was also extended to the King Airs.

August 30, 1989. Beaton and Sims sailed the San Francisco Bay. The winds were, at times, calm, and the tide was running out. Fighting the tide with little wind, the two sailors were stuck a few times near or under the Oakland side of the Bay Bridge!

Bay Bridge Oakland side, August 30, 1989.

On October 17, 1989, the Loma-Prieta earthquake caused significant damage to the San Francisco Bay area and the Bay Bridge.

Collapsed section of the Bay Bridge!
Photo by C.E. Meyer of the U.S. Geographical Survey

The earthquake also caused the collapse of a two-tiered section of Interstate 880. Beaton and other pilots traveled this route when sailing.

Collapsed section of Interstate 880
Photo by H.G. Wilshire of the U.S. Geographical Survey

Chapter Six: The 1990s. A Changing Landscape

Flight operations had primarily become routine at the start of the 90's. Flights to the subsidiaries of Dillon Co's Inc. come like clockwork. The long-range trips are mostly in the Sabreliner, mid-range in the Citation, and short-range in the King Airs. An F-90 King Air replaced the E-90 King Air in early 1990. The cabin size resembles the E model but has a T-tail and more powerful engines. The pilots must be trained in its operation. The larger Model 200 King Air is still in service.

Beechcraft Model F-90
Photo by Acroterion 🔗 #12

Two vice presidents now oversaw the convenience store division. Each are assigned to different store operations. The two VPs are Bill Bell, who heads the western group, and Bob Meyers, who oversees the eastern group.

January 1990. In appreciation of the convenience stores sales of its products, Miller Brewing Co. awards the two VPs two tickets each to attend Super Bowl XXIV in New Orleans. The teams were the Denver Broncos and the San Francisco 49ers. Whether their wives did not want to attend is unknown, but a business flight was scheduled to New Orleans on game day. One ticket was given to the pilot of the trip and one to Sam Sharp, President of Loaf and Jug of Colorado, a big Broncos fan.

Sims, as Chief Pilot, assigned himself as the pilot! Sam Sharp paid his way to New Orleans and met the other three at the Super Dome. Meyer and Bell are seated in Miller's VIP box, while Sharp and Sims are in good stadium seating near the 50-yard line. The game is a bust for the Broncos and the most lop-sided Superbowl ever. The final score was San Francisco 55, Denver 10.

After the game, Sharp and Sims were invited to the Miller Brewing hospitality suite for a buffet dinner with Meyers and Bell. Sims follows Sharp in the buffet line. Behind Sims is a tall, young blond woman who is very attractive. She is also friendly and starts conversing with Sims about the game. She is accompanied by an equally friendly guy, and the three share remarks about the highlights and lowlights of the game.

Upon returning to the table to join the group, Bell asks Sims, "Do you know who that girl is you were talking to in the buffet line?" Sims replies, "No, but she was gorgeous!" Bell then tells Sims, "That gorgeous girl is Daryl Hannah, the movie star!" "Holy Crap" replies Sims and asks, "Who was the guy she was with?" No one at the table recognized him.

**Daryl Hannah and Jackson Browne.
Photo by Alan Light** 🔗 **#13**

Long after retiring, Sims learned that the guy was musician/songwriter/singer Jackson Browne. He and Hannah were an item from 1987 to 1992.

August 1990. Collins Industries sold their B100 King Air, and Gary Crow returned to Koch Industries. Wells hires Max Murray.

1991. The Frys begin to use their Sabreliner more often. Sims and Hephner were the only pilots rated in the Sabres. Hephner declares himself Chief Pilot for the Fry's and appoints Karen Anderson as First Officer. Sims and Hephner discuss type rating another pilot in the Sabres. Lincoln Hall has been with City Markets since 1974, but answers to Sims and Hephner at Wells.

They asked Hall if he would like to relocate to Hutchinson and become type-rated in the Sabreliner. He consulted with his family, and they accepted the offer together. He subsequently moved to Hutchinson in August 0f 91.

Sims informed Don Beaton of the decision to bring Hall to Hutchinson due to his seniority with the Company. This conversation was tough for Sims because of Beaton's loyalty and contributions to the Flight Dept. Sims knew Beaton would be disappointed and hoped Beaton would not leave the Company. Fortunately for Sims and the Company, Beaton stayed.

1992. Ace buys a Marchetti F260D. It is an Italian-built 2-seat sport plane certified in the aerobatic category. It is used by many countries' Air Forces in training fighter pilots!

Ace takes his grandson Henry Platts for a ride on Henry's 7th Birthday!

Henry's mother, Diane, knew of Ace's antics in this plane and observed the flight with binoculars. Henry remembers his grandfather telling him, "A parachute is required for this flight, but you are too small to wear it." The requirement was dismissed, and off they went!

Ace offered the use of the Marchetti to all company pilots. They only had to pay for the fuel used. The airplane was fun to fly, and everyone took advantage of Ace's generosity!

Hephner hired an aerobatics flight instructor and learned to perform many maneuvers. Hephner sometimes would take Wells Aircraft customers for a thrill ride in the Marchetti. Most enjoyed the ride, but some were scared witless!

May 1993. Ray Milsap was hired as a contract pilot. Milsap, a retired Marine military pilot, flew F-4 Phantom fighters in two tours in Vietnam. Milsap was a seasoned pilot with many hours in the T-39, the military version of the Sabreliner.

July, 1993. Gary Crow will return to Wells Aircraft as a full-time pilot. Although he is typed in the Sabreliner series, he does not currently act as Pilot In Command. However, in August of that year, he obtained his type rating in the Cessna 500 series.

Crow and Sims are both gearheads interested in old cars and trucks. The two had found many salvage yards in the desert southwest in past years. On overnight trips to the area, they would take a portable cooler from the airplane, buy a six-pack of beer, and scour salvage yards for rust-free treasures!

1994. Some pilots express their concerns about Hephner's judgment in instrument flying conditions. On one occasion, a co-pilot reports that Hephner busted minimums on a non-precision approach to Muskogee OK. On another, a co-pilot reports that Hephner flew through a final approach localizer. He banked the airplane steeply and put excessive back pressure on the control yoke in his attempt to get back to it. That co-pilot feared Hephner might pull the wings off or induce a low-altitude accelerated stall!

Sims tried tactfully to talk to Hephner about the events without revealing with whom, where, or when they occurred. Sims was met with rebuke. Hephner said, "I know what I'm doing, and there was no danger in my actions!"

Technically, Hephner became Sims' boss when Haines passed away and did not like Sims very much. Hephner avoided flying with Sims to prevent criticism of his performance. Sims is beginning to suspect Hephner is developing "BPS" (Bullet Proof Syndrome) and tells pilots who fly with him to be vigilant and tactfully correct any deviations Hephner may make!

May 1994: Ace turns 70, the mandatory retirement age for Kroger executives. With Ace's retirement, James Hephner became President of Wells Aircraft Inc.

June 1994. The Dillon Sabreliner and Citation are dispatched to Buffalo, NY. The Flight crews take advantage of the opportunity to visit Niagara Falls.

**From left: Don Beaton, Max Murray, and Lincoln Hall.
On the American side of Niagara Falls.**

July 1994. Sims and Crow are on a trip to Galveston, TX. While securing the airplane, they spot their old Howard 500, N277X. It sits next to one of the Lone Star Flight Museum restoration hangars. It appears to have been scavenged for parts. The museum has a PV-2 "Harpoon," which the Howard shares some components.

The cabin door is not locked on the 500, Sims and Crow enter the airplane. The interior has been gutted, and tie-down rings have been installed on the floor. It is believed the airplane was used as a drug smuggling mule at some time. The instrument panel was missing some gauges and navigation instruments. What a sad ending for such a majestic and unique airplane!

June 22, 1995. Tragedy strikes the Convenience Stores division of Dillon Co's Inc. Sims received a call from David Dillon late that afternoon saying, "We need to make an emergency flight to Crestview, FL, early tomorrow morning. Bob Meyers and the president of Tom Thumb Stores have been killed in an automobile accident!"

Don Beaton had flown Meyers to Crestview earlier that day. Sims contacts Beaton at his motel, informs him of the situation, and tells him to stand by for further instructions when Mr. Dillon arrives in the morning.

Disbelief and sadness permeate the following day as condolences are expressed, and plans for the next steps are made. When released, Beaton will fly Mr. Meyer's belongings back to Hutchinson. Sims and his co-pilot will remain until Mr. Dillon concludes his unpleasant tasks.

Not long after Meyers's tragic death, Bell retires. Replacing both as vice president of all convenience store operations is Robert "Bob" Moeder. Moeder has been a long-time manager and vice president of various Dillon Co's Inc. subsidiaries, including Kwik Shops convenience store operations.

Not long after the unfortunate events in Crestview, Hephner and Hall were on a return trip from Cincinnati. David Dillon is among the passengers. There are building storms along the route, with one directly in front of the flight. Hall asks Hephner, the pilot flying, if he wants to deviate around the building storm. Hephner confidently replies, "No, we will top that build-up!"

Well, they did not. Hephner flew directly into the building storm, experiencing severe turbulence and a lightning strike! Hall tells Sims of the encounter and how frightened he and the passengers were. Sims calls David Dillon and asks him what he felt about the experience. Dillon confirmed that he was scared of what might happen during the encounter.

Sims requests and is granted a meeting with Dillon to discuss Hephner's behavior. Sims tells Dillon about Hephner's "Bullet Proof Syndrome," believing nothing terrible can happen to him. Also, it has come to Sims' attention that Hephner has run afoul of the FAA Air Traffic Controllers in Wichita and Hutchinson with demands of special treatment over other flyers. The FAA is looking for any reason to file non-compliance charges against Hephner.

Sims recommends Hephner be grounded for safety's sake and Hephner's reputation. Dillon agrees that he and Sims meet with Hephner and recount the events of concern to him and that they both agree he should give up his pilot duties.

The meeting was painful for all parties but particularly for Hephner because he was a proud man. But he respected the decision, gave up flying, and focused on Wells Aircraft's business operations.

Ray Milsap took over as Captain of the Fry Sabreliner.

Later that year, David Dillon became President of Kroger. Warren Bryant becomes President and CEO of Dillon Co's Inc.

The F-90 King Air is found to be just as costly to operate as the 200 model. The decision is made to replace it with a Beech model 58 "Baron" for short-range flights. It is a light, non-turbine twin-engine airplane with seating for a pilot and five passengers. If flown at full passenger capacity, they would know each other well at the end of the flight!

Beechcraft B-58 Baron
Photo by James 🔗 #14

April 1996. Lincoln Hall resigned and took a position with Westar Energy of Kansas City. Don Beaton is type-rated in the Sabreliner. Another young local, Doug Mann, is hired as a pilot. Mann quickly assimilates into the flight dept.

Summer 1996. The FAA issued a notice of change in the Hutchinson navigation and approach facilities. The FAA proposes moving the Hutchinson VOR nav-aid to the northwest around Sterling or Lyons, KS. Also in the plan is de-commissioning and removal of some of the instrument approach facilities at the Hutchinson Municipal Airport..

Learning of this proposal, Wells Aircraft and Sims are spearheading a campaign to keep the facilities as they are. They are crucial in keeping

Hutchinson Municipal Airport an all-weather airport, a vital asset to the city's commerce.

A petition in opposition to the proposed changes was composed. Sims then contacts all gen-av manufacturers of Wichita, Flight Safety Int. Wichita and Vance Air Force Base in Enid, OK., all utilize the Hutchinson facilities. All entities agree to sign the petition with comments on why they are in opposition.

The campaign was successful, and the proposal was withdrawn!

Hephner's crusty management style is becoming a concern for some employees. They are threatened with termination for indiscretions they feel are unjustified. Hephner had an intense glare, and if aimed at you, you knew you were in trouble!

At one point, a hurricane threatened the east coast of Florida. One of the mechanics said, "Let's just send Hephner down there, put him on the beach, and have him glare at it; it won't dare come ashore!"

Sims is informed of this behavior, with some employees threatening to quit after years of loyal service. Sims feels compelled to notify Bryant of the situation. Bryant suggests some management training for Hephner which may help. Bryant jokingly tells Sims, "We'll find a 'Charm School' to send him to!" They did, it helped!

1997. Max Murray retires. Jennifer Wuertz of McPherson, KS, replaced Murry. Jennifer became the first full-time female pilot and acts as "Pilot In Command" for Dillon Co's Inc. She quickly gains her peers' respect and her passengers' confidence!

After passengers complained about cramped space and difficulty entering and exiting it, the Beech Baron was replaced by a C-90B King Air.

The Dillon fleet is all cabin class and turbine-powered, much to the passengers' delight!

1998. Fred Meyer Super Markets of Hillsborough, OR, merged with the Kroger Company. Meyer is a large western United States company similar in operational practices to Dillon Co's Inc., which is comprised of many subsidiary grocery chains.

Richard "Dick" Dillon turns 70 and retires.

Jim Hephner retires. Sims once again declined to become President of Wells Aircraft and recommended Gary Crow take the position. Crow became the third president of Wells Aircraft.

Gary Crow, left, and his crew of mechanics in 1998.

1999. Warren Bryant is named President of Fred Meyer Stores, and Paul Scutt is named President of Dillon Co's Inc.

The Fry's sons built a business of their own, Fry's Electronics, which specialized in computer-related merchandise. They convinced their parents to move the Sabreliner to southern California, where most of their business was. They repaint the airplane in Airforce trim and have fun flying it to different aviation events!

The Fry's Sabreliner after repaint!

Noise restrictions are implemented at some airports where Dillon Co.'s Sabreliners operate, banning the aircraft from landing and taking off. Noise restrictions are anticipated at more airports, necessitating the use of a quieter airplane.

The Sabreliner was a great flying airplane but was powered by straight turbo-jet engines, which were very noisy. On a still winter morning, it could be heard from miles away on take-off!

The Citation was powered by a turbo-fan engine, which is much quieter. The decision was made to trade the Sabreliner for a Citation II. The "Two" has a larger cabin, extended range, and more speed than the "One SP" but is not as fast as the Sabre.

The Dillon Cessna Citation II – N255TC

Crow was very customer-oriented and was always looking to find ways to drum up business. One of those ways was having customer appreciation days from time to time. Often having a fly-in breakfast for his customers.

Customer Appreciation Breakfast

L to R: Roger Stroberg, John Bornholt, Mike Hildebrand, Jared Bornholt and Gary Bornholt.

Chapter Seven: The New Millennia

Major Change

2000. The Kroger Company management and the Board of Directors decided to re-organize the company—Dillon Co's. Inc was dissolved, its components were divided into Kroger East, Central, or West. Most Dillon Co's Inc. Super Markets are now in Kroger West. All convenience stores are now Kroger Central, and Moeder is named Kroger Central President.

Group photo of Dillon Co's. Inc. employees before closing. The Flight Dept. principals are included.

With the end of Dillon Co.'s. Inc., technically, the Dillon Flight Dept. no longer existed. The airplanes now belonged to Kroger, and Kroger employed the pilots.

The King Air and Citation I SP are sold off. The Citation II remains in Hutchinson at Wells Aircraft, now a Kroger subsidiary. Kroger Central is headquartered in Hutchinson and oversees the Convenience Store Divisions. Moeder was promoted to president of the Indianapolis IN. Kroger Marketing Area. Van Tarver, formerly of Quik Stops, CA., is named President of Kroger Central.

Mr. T is now in charge of the Citation II and the pilots. Mr. T has mellowed by this time and did not impose many changes to the Kroger Central flight department operation out of respect for Wells Aircraft and the pilots.

Ironically, Doug Mann resigned and went to Trans World Airlines.

2000. Crow was diagnosed with Parkinson's disease and retired from his flying duties.

A second female pilot is hired. Nancy Skinner of Wichita joins the flight department and is accepted as Jennifer Wuertz was.

2001. Dillons Stores Division acquires Baker's Supermarkets of Omaha, NE, and Food4Less of Freemont, NE.

Early summer 2001, Sims announced his retirement at the end of August. Coincidentally, Jennifer Wuertz announces she is pregnant with her first child and will resign at about the same time!

Sims will take his last flight as a full-time employee on August 30/31 to Indianapolis, IN., with Skinner as his FO. Skinner was asked to fly to Indy as Sims wanted to fly home on his last trip. For some reason, Skinner was reluctant to do so but relented.

After landing on return to Hutchinson and turning to taxi to Wells, Sims was surprised by the number of Dillon Co's, Wells Aircraft, family, and other well-wishers waiting to welcome him home. There were tables set up in Hangar 2 with a barbeque banquet prepared by Harold Ryan, retired Director of HR Dillon Co's. and John Baldwin, retired President of Dillon Stores Div. Was this the reason for Skinner's reluctance? Because the pilot not flying is usually the first person to exit the aircraft!

"Surprise!! Surprise!!!"

During the evening, many people spoke of their flying experiences with Sims. Some with praise and others with amusing tales! But the biggest surprise was learning that by the generosity of the Dillons and others, Crow had arranged for Sims a flight in a B-17 from Fayetteville, AR., to Hutchinson in late Sept. They also presented him with a scale model of the B-17 "Sentimental Journey" in which he flew.

Then 911 happens! This event ended Doug Mann's airline aspirations, and he rejoined Dillon/Kroger.

Friday, Sept. 28, 2001. Karen Anderson donates her time and airplane to fly Sims to Fayetteville, AR. so that he can fly to Hutchinson on the B-17 "Sentimental Journey." Sims gets to manipulate the bomber's controls for a while, fulfilling his childhood dream!

"Two Thumbs Up" on arrival in Hutch!

Gary Crow greets an ecstatic Sims!

Jan. 2002. Kroger aims to divest Wells Aircraft, which Gary Crow purchased, to maintain the business as a locally owned entity. Moeder played a crucial role in facilitating the negotiations between Kroger and Crow.

Ms. Skinner is now the senior pilot in Hutchinson and answers directly to Mr. T, who had again become more demanding of the Hutchinson flight operations.

Mr. Tarver was not happy with the speed of Citation II, which is around 100 MPH slower than the Sabreliner. Kroger is shutting down its Smiths Markets in Salt Lake City, Utah, Flight department. They have operated a Lear Jet Model 35 which is much faster than the Citation. The Lear is moved to Hutchinson, and the Citation sold.

Needing a seasoned Lear pilot, Rick Rogers is hired and named Chief Pilot. Rogers also knows how to placate Mr. T's demands as well! Ms. Skinner is not upset with this and is relieved that she no longer has to deal with Mr. T.

With the acquisition of Bakers and Food-4-Less of Nebraska, Dillon Stores Div.contracts a King Air when needed from Wichita to visit the Nebraska stores. It was crewed by its owner and one of Kroger's pilots.

In 2004, Terry Benton comes on board as a pilot.

Nov. 2004. Due in part to failing health and shrinking revenue, Gary Crow is forced to sell Wells Aircraft Inc. Wells was bought by Don Rogers (no known relation to Rick Rogers) in conjunction with Stutzman Co. Stutzman operates a flower and plant nursery, a refuse pickup service, and farming in the Hutchinson area.

August 2005. Doug Mann moves to Cessna Aircraft as a Citation production test pilot. He is still with Textron/Cessna as of the time of this writing.

This leaves Rick Rogers, Nancy Skinner, and Terry Benton to crew the Lear. At some point, a fourth pilot, Lionel Perez, was hired to help crew the Lear. These four, plus mechanic, Lew Tomac, are the Kroger Central Flight Dept personnel. Ms. Skinner resignes in 2012.

Van Tarver announced his retirement in early 2014. Kroger decides not to replace him in Hutchinson. Instead, they assign two Kroger VPs based in Cincinnati to carry out their duties.

The Kroger Central Flight Dept. is no longer needed with this development. Kroger shut down this Department on Monday, March 23, 2014.

The Lear Jet is flown to Cincinnati on Thursday, March 27th, for the final time.

Friday, March 28, 2014: The Hutchinson News ran a nearly full front-page article and a bold headline that reads, "An era folds its wings!"

2014: David Dillon retires as CEO and Board Chairman of Kroger Co. David spends his last day in service to the Kroger Co. doing the job where he began his career, as a grocery bagger and carry-out boy at a small Dillons store at the corner of 14th Ave. and Main Street in Hutchinson, KS.

THE LAST DAY

Don Rogers, left, president of Wells Aircraft, walks with Chief Pilot Rick Rogers, mechanic Lew Tomac and Line Captain Terry Benton toward the Learjet 35 on Thursday morning as the plane makes its final flight from Hutchinson. Kroger Aviation has closed its Hutchinson base of operation and will no longer fly Dillons Company executives out of Hutchinson.

Courtesy of The Hutchinson News

The Dillon organization contributed significantly to the aviation industry and served the community of Hutchinson for eight decades from the late 1940s to 2014.

The Lear Jet's last flight marked a sad day for everyone involved with Dillon Co's and Wells Aircraft.

Epilogue

The Major Players

1. Ace Dillon: No matter who held the title of "Chief Pilot," as long as Ace was engaged as an officer of the company, he was "THE" Chief Pilot! As in his business acumen, Ace recognized talent and delegated responsibility to those he knew would carry it out as he would. One always knew where they stood with Ace. If he was displeased, he didn't hesitate to let you know. If he arrived for a trip without greeting you, he had something on his mind: <u>Do Not Disturb</u>! When greeting you with a smile, all is well with the world. Ace loved automobiles and would bring new ones he had bought to Wells. He would let those employees he knew were 'gear heads' take them for a spin with the radio playing Rock and Roll music, his favorite!

2. Bill Haines: Not only was he an excellent pilot, but he was quite an entrepreneur. In just a few years, he took Wells Aircraft Inc. from a local service company to a nationwide company. Then, Wells Aircraft would have a worldwide presence a few years after that. Haines was well-liked by his employees, who recognized and applauded their achievements. He would take new pilots under his wing, guiding them and instilling confidence by letting them fly "left seat" in the larger, more complex airplanes. He served for 30 years.

3. Jim Hephner: Mechanically talented, he could analyze a seemingly complex problem quickly and come up with a solution equally quickly. He devised modifications or fixes for airplanes that required a Standard Type Certificate for the mod/fix to be applied to its Airworthiness Certificate. As a pilot, he had limited experience. His pilot-in-command time was mainly made on test flights of those airplanes that didn't require a type rating. After he was typed in the Sabre and named Vice President of Wells Aircraft, he began gaining experience in the corporate flying environment. Despite his "Crusty" management style, he was quite a "Softy" at times. He served for 34 years.

4. Dean Wedman: Promoted to Service Manager in Hephner's Place. Highly skilled and just as capable and dedicated to safety as Hephner but with a softer management style. Yet conscientious of his Responsibilities. A Skycraft Transfer, Dean was Wells Aircraft Inc.'s longest-serving employee, along with Dillon Co's Inc., and the Kroger Co. In service for 37 years.

5. Gary Crow: Although he left Wells for a period, he was a loyal member of the flight department for years after his return. Well-liked and respected by his peers, Crow became the Standard Bearer of Wells Aircraft Inc., eventually becoming President and then the business owner. After selling Wells and suffering a debilitating ailment, Crow did not give up his love for aviation. He went to work for Flight Safety as a 'systems instructor' in Wichita. He served for a total of 19 years.

6. Mike Sims: Not as well-liked as Haines or Crow, Sims loved the feel of flight and flying. Often "hogging" the left seat of the Beech 18's, DC-3's, and the Sabreliners, his favorites! He, however, was conscientious of his position. He cared for his pilots' well-being, proficiency, and passengers' safety. He served for 33 years.

Valued Long Time Members

7. Lincoln Hall: Hired as a pilot for City Markets of Grand Junction, CO. Hall was a young but experienced Mountain Pilot. Always safety conscious, Hall would pester Haines for better-performing airplanes for mountain flying. He served for 21 years.

8. Don Beaton: Committed and loyal to the company, he was a skilled and knowledgeable pilot, flight instructor, and examiner. Haines and Sims never worried when Beaton commanded a trip. He served for 20 years.

9. Karen Anderson: As a contract pilot, Anderson was the first female crew member to serve as a First Officer in the Dillon Flight Department beginning in 1985. Had she become a full-time employee when she first started, she may have been qualified as Captain. She served the Dillon Cos and the Fry family for 20+ years.

10. Ray Milsap: As a contract pilot, Milsap also served the Dillon Co's and the Fry's family for many years. He was a fill-in pilot as Captain on the Sabreliners of Dillon Co's Inc. and Fry's.

External Links↗

Photos so denoted are licensed under Creative Commons (©) or Wikipedia Commons (🌐).

1: P-47 by Tim Felce ©①③ Share Alike 2.0 Generic (https://creativecommons.org/licenses/by-sa/2.0/deed.en) License

2: Piper J-3 by Bill Larkins ©①③ Shre Alike 2.0 Generic (https://creativecommons.org/licenses/by-sa/2.0/deed.en) License

3: 310 by Allen Wilson ©①③ Share Alike 2.0 Generic (https://creativecommons.org/licenses/by-sa/2.0/deed.en) License

4: G-1 by Bill Larkins ©①③ .Share Alike 2.0 Generic (https://creativecommons.org/licenses/by-sa/2.0/deed.en) License

5: Jenny by Bill Larkins ©①③ Share Alike 2.0 Generic (https://creativecommons.org/licenses/by-sa/2.0/deed.en) License

6: Citation 500 by Rob Hodgkins ©①③ Share Alike 2.0 Generic (https://creativecommons.org/licenses/by-sa/2.0/deed.en) License

7: B-18 Tri Gear by aeroprints ©①③ Share Alike 3.0 Unported (https://creativecommons.org/licenses/by-sa/3.0/deed.en)& (http://www.aeroprints.com)

8: 340 by Bill Larkins ©①③ Share Alike 2.0 Generic (https://creativecommons.org/licenses/by-sa/2.0/deed.en) License

9: 421B by Acroterion ©①③ Share Alike 4.0 International(https://creativecommons.org/licenses/by-sa/4.0/deed.en) License

10: 402B by SDASM 🌐 (https://commons.wikipedia.org/wiki/File:Cessna_402_II.jpg), scroll down for license info.

11: Beech 90 series by Acroterion ©①③ Share Alike 4.0 International (https://creativecommons.org/licenses/by-sa/4.0/deed.en) License

12: Beech F-90 by Acroterion ⓒⓘⓢ Share Alike 4.0 International (https://creativecommons.org/licenses/by-sa/4.0/deed.en) License

13: Hanna & Browne by Alan Light ⓒⓘⓢ Share Alike 2.0 Generic (https://creativecommons.org/licenses/by-sa/2.0/deed.en) License

14: Baron by James ⓒⓘⓢ Share Alike 2.0 Generic (https://creativecommons.org/licenses/by-sa/2.0/deed.en) License

www.ingramcontent.com/pod-product-compliance
Lightning Source LLC
Chambersburg PA
CBHW041143110526
44590CB00027B/4109